For my parents — with all my love and thanks

Healthy Wine
and Beer Making

Peter McCall

ARGUS BOOKS

Argus Books Limited
Wolsey House
Wolsey Road
Hemel Hempstead
Hertfordshire HP2 4SS

First published by Argus Books 1988
© Peter McCall 1988

ISBN 0 85242 937 1

All rights reserved. No part of this publication may be reproduced in any form, by print, photography, microfilm or any other means without written permission from the publisher.

Phototypesetting by En to En Typesetters, Tunbridge Wells, Kent, TN2 3XD
Printed and bound by LR Printing Services Limited, Manor Royal, Crawley, West Sussex, RH10 2QN, England

Contents

List of Tables

Preface

The aim of this book is to provide a simple guide to winemaking and brewing using only natural ingredients while endeavouring to aid health at the same time. Unfortunately, we cannot produce cures for all ills, nor can we say that these recipes and suggestions will be of benefit. But they should, if properly used, and above all not abused, do you no harm.

However, there is one important point which should be stated at the outset. *Should you suffer from any medical condition — particularly if you need to take any medication — do not consume alcohol without consulting your doctor or pharmacist.* In many cases alcohol is positively banned from your diet if you are taking treatment of any sort.

After discussing the relationship between health and winemaking and brewing, we will look at various parts of the body, and see how we can, firstly, not abuse it with alcohol and secondly, possibly help it with recipes based on old herbal remedies.

The number of herbs in medicinal use, in Europe alone, runs into many hundreds. In order to keep the book within manageable proportions, only those used in winemaking and brewing are mentioned. I have not used the most recent editon of *Martindale's Pharmacopoeia* because most of the herb and plant references have been deleted. Thus, mention of 'recent' references relate to the 25th Edition of 1967.

I hope that by the end of this book you will be spurred on to try some of these recipes and will enjoy a healthy life with the occasional glass of beer or wine by your side.

Acknowledgements

As always my thanks go to all those whose help made sure this book was finished — and errors and omissions corrected or inserted.

For fifteen years now, I have relied upon one of the best critics I know — my father. He has the infuriating knack of invariably pointing out errors — of grammar, punctuation, English, fact — as well as our common ground, medicine. To him, above all others, I owe an immense debt of gratitude in checking, not only this manuscript, but every book I have written.

I must record, also, my thanks to Dr Joe Baker who has furnished much recent data on herbs and medicine, as well as the librarian at the Royal Berkshire Hospital Postgraduate Centre who searched indefatigably for references.

To HMSO for permission to reprint extracts from *The Composition of Foodstuffs*.

Finally, my appreciation to all at *Argus Books* who put up with disaster and delays while ever providing cheerful help.

Other books by Peter McCall

Winemaker's Dictionary, *Argus Books*
Brewer's Dictionary, *Argus Books*

McCall's Greyfriars Guide, *Howard Baker Press*

1 Friend or Foe?

The first issue to be settled is whether or not we can allow ourselves to drink. Later in the book we shall see how much can be permitted.

Today, there is an increasing awareness of the dangers of excessive drinking. Only a few years ago, the definition of moderate drinking was up to, and including, seventeen drinks per day! Today, that is considered, quite correctly, massively excessive. Recent suggestions as to the limits of sensible drinking are up to fourteen drinks *per week*. It is, however, not a good idea to drink every day but rather to have a couple of 'days off' each week. Similarly, modern thought rejects the idea of 'binges'.

Obviously, certain medical conditions prohibit the consumption of alcohol. If you are taking any medication, it is wise – and often essential – to avoid alcohol. The medicine you are taking may be prevented from working if you drink at the same time. For example:

> Some drugs for illnesses such as depression will have dire effects if you consume alcohol.

> If pregnant, it is sensible for the sake of your child-to-be, not to drink. There is also a recent suggestion that some herbal preparations are best avoided during this time.

> For the diabetic, some tablets used in treating the condition can actually make the condition worse if you take alcohol.

From these few examples, it is obvious that care needs to be exercised in any medical context when it comes to drinking. Ask your doctor if you may drink with the pills he has just given you and he is most likely to advise you to stay away from drink until the treatment is finished. It is most important to follow his instructions to the letter.

It is when we come to examine the social side of drinking that we experience the greatest difficulty. For, when faced with 'peer pressure' or trying to make a sale at work, or feeling down, it is very easy to give in and take too much alcohol. It is therefore necessary to try to impose limits on your drinking, not only in the number of drinks consumed but also in the amount of alcohol itself that you ingest.

Alcohol is not, as thought by many people, a lifter of mood; it is, in fact, a depressant. The cheerfulness experienced by many people is actually the lifting of barriers imposed by social constraints or the relaxation of inhibitions by the first action of alcohol on the brain.

Like so many substances in widespread use today, (tea, coffee, cocoa), alcohol is capable of misuse. Figures quoted for this abuse vary widely from almost none, up to 7-8% of the population. Just what the true figure is is impossible to say because problem drinkers tend to hide their behaviour and especially their drinking habits. It is a fact that, when asked about their drinking and smoking habits, most people will always give an answer way below the truth.

The person who needs a drink first thing in the morning needs medical help more than he or she needs alcohol. The drinker who cannot remember what happened the previous evening, or whose work record is suffering through late arrivals, early departures, or deteriorating work performance, must also seek medical help.

Alcohol is a social drug. If used in moderation and in appropriate conditions there is little or no harm attachable to it.

For the average 'drinker', who has the occasional pint of beer or glass of wine with Sunday lunch or to celebrate an anniversary, there is only pleasure to be obtained from his favourite tipple. This is certainly my own belief.

Historically speaking, wine has always played an important part in medicine and in the eighteenth century it was in widespread use as an anaesthetic.

I have a medical textbook dated 1660. In the chapter on diet, wine is mentioned as one of the beverages available to man. There is no suggestion as to therapeutic benefits obtainable from it nor, indeed, the harms. Chinese recipes for medicinal wines (more accurately they are infusions of fruit or herbs in rice wine) claim benefits for a wide range of conditions. Their origins are lost in antiquity, and the recipes for similar conditions vary according to the part of that country from which the recipe originates.

The British Pharmacopoeia of 1890 lists among the medicinal wines *Antimony* as a Diaphoretic (or inducer of sweating); *Aloes* for digestive upsets; and *Colchicum* as being good for the kidneys. However, these particular ingredients are not recommended for the home winemaker as they contain poisonous substances. Everyone knows of the *Tonic Wines* containing iron; they are said to be good for anaemia as well as 'fortifying' the drinker (if old enough!).

What, if anything, can we glean from this? In prehistory alcohol was, probably, a magical potion. The changing of honey, grain, or fruit from everyday edible crops into alcoholic drinks must have seemed nothing short of miraculous to early man. Even in the middle ages, yeast was known as *Goddisgoode* — a name based upon mystic perceptions of fermentation. From this basic, unscientific worship of fermentation could have come the investing of the products of fermentation with magical powers. After all, did not the consumption of large quantities result in strange behaviour? If it was then noticed that consumption of small portions of a particular herb wine aided the sick to recover, the beginnings of therapeutics had been discovered.

Throughout the early millennia of man's time on earth, knowledge would have been accumulated about the effects — beneficial and harmful — of different substances on man. True, there was as yet no scientific basis for what were, in effect, beliefs; but, when we look at many of today's drugs and realise that they were developed from plants used by the witch doctor or Wise Woman for thousands of years, one can only marvel at primitive man's ability to learn and, indeed, to treat successfully so many complaints. As knowledge about all subjects spread, so too did the use of these early drugs.

By the early part of our era, alcohol had become much more available and was widely consumed, both for its intoxicating effects and its use as the basis for many medicines.

Throughout the Middle Ages in Europe, the Monasteries were the seats of all knowledge: religious, secular, and medical. Most universities were founded by religious orders as centres of education. In the Herbarium of the monasteries the Brother

Herbalist prepared wines. He also tended the herb garden wherein he grew the valuable plants (many brought from abroad by visiting brothers) from which he prepared the treatments of the day, either by fermentation or by infusion. Obviously, many preparations were made using other methods but, from the fermentative point of view, these are the methods of use.

Using fermentative techniques the Herbalist would make, for example, a *Tansy Wine* for use as a tonic. Using infusion methods, he might take a wine and then place a bag of herbs in it to extract their active substances.

These methods of preparing drugs continued until recently. Now we have science to create, prepare and purify medicines. But, before the chemist of today, there were only very few methods of preparing compounds: heat, fermentation, crushing, and alcoholic extraction. Of these, alcohol was one of the most important.

Thus, it is clear how important the place of medicinal wines is in the old Pharmacopoeiae and why the Wise Woman of the village played such a large part in the health of the community.

Before the rise of medicine as a profession, the Wise Woman was either almost deified for her skill or reviled as a witch, depending on her success or failure. Going back to the religious basis for medicine it is easy to understand this. If a patient recovered was this not the hand of God? Alternatively, should the patient worsen or die, this must mean the hand of the Devil — and his handmaiden was a witch. To add credence to this belief, the locals would point to the foul smells created as she brewed her mischief, her lonely existence and her long absences (collecting plants, not cavorting with Lucifer). But, they would all come to her for a posset to ward off the ague, a love philtre, or a potion to make the cow give more milk. Despite their apparent beliefs, the people always made good use of her.

As we have already seen, alcohol and herbs can play a large part in the sustenance of good health. And who is to say that, given the use of non-toxic ingredients, they are not as effective as some of the remedies otherwise available even today? But, and this is vital, excess will do no good. The belief that twice as much will do twice as much good is a philosophy to be avoided.

2 The Bitter-Sweet Controversy

At the root of the efforts to achieve 'Healthy Wines and Beers', lies the premise that it is sensible, if not imperative, to avoid 'sugars', which may at first appear odd, since there seems little doubt that man has always had a sweet tooth. This can be deduced from the presence of, and the types of, taste-buds we have on our tongues. These are four: sweet, sour, salt, and bitter. To these we must add the sense of smell, for much tasting is done by the nose.

We are most sensitive to sour and bitter tastes: salt and sweet substances need to be present in larger quantities to stimulate taste buds. It may be that at least part of man's predilection for things sweet derives from the fact that many poisonous substances are bitter to taste. From this develops the (dangerous) theory and folk lore that sweet fruits are harmless and then, probably, the idea that they are positively beneficial to man.

In prehistoric times, and indeed until comparatively recently, honey and ripe fruit were the 'sweets' of the day. From the fermentative angle, grains are probably the origins of alcohol. The Chinese have records dating back to 1500 BC giving accounts of wine drinking and distillation, as well as surviving drinking utensils. As the vine did not reach China until much later, they must have fermented other fruit and grain, including millet.

There is plenty of evidence to show that grapes were dried (thus creating a store of raisins) and were also made into wine in the Middle Eastern countries. Minoan Crete, too, is known to have cultivated the grape. Its cultivation spread eastwards through the ages, presumably *via* successive invasions, until the Chinese learned about the vine in 128 BC.

Cereals were developed 'locally' by each culture, depending on local varieties and climate. Basically, the different cereal crops were distinguishable by about 1200 BC. From these, the various local variations on beer were developed around the world.

It is unclear whether, as claimed by many experts, mead is the oldest fermented drink known to man. It is, however, quite likely to have been the earliest natural produce used regularly for the express purpose of making alcoholic beverages. Other ingredients, being required for foodstuffs, perhaps only fermented by mistake — unless there was a seasonal glut, in which case the surplus could be used for a 'brew up'!

Whatever the case, it is certain that honey was an early addition to man's diet, its sweetness and food value making it a prize discovery to a nomadic tribesman. This adds support to the argument that mead was man's first fermentation, because grains were most probably not fermented until he had a more settled life style. Whatever the case, cave paintings exist showing early man collecting honey.

Later, *Hyppocras,* made from fermented grape juice and honey, with added herbs, was enjoyed and revered by the Ancient Greeks.

During the early part of the first millenium, fermented honey in one form or another was the staple fermented drink of most of Northern Europe for special occasions. As the culture of southern Europe spread north under the influence of Christianity, so too did the culture of wine.

Honey was not only used for fermentation, it was also the chief sweetening agent in use until the advent of 'sugar' as the product of the sugar cane became known. The word derives from the Old French *çucre,* which in turn comes from Greek *sacchar* via the Latin *saccharon.* This latter appears in the Natural History by Pliny the elder; so that sugar cane was at least known about in Italy in the first seventy years AD, and in Greece before that date. Lucan, a contemporary of Nero, also mentions saccharon in reference to 'These strange people who suck the sweet juice of the sugar-cane. . . .' Here, Lucan is talking about the Brahmins of Northern India.

It seems that the sugar cane evolved in Oceania from whence it spread to India and Africa. Possibly Alexander the Great brought samples back with him from his failed conquest of India, a possibility given credence by the reference in Lucan.

For many hundreds of years, cane sugar was an expensive luxury — even in the 13th Century King Henry III of England had problems in finding as much as 3 lbs for a banquet. The major reason for trade with The Barbary Coast, now Morocco, in the 16th Century was almost entirely due to the demand for sugar.

With the discovery and opening up of the New World in the Middle Ages came the development of the sugar industry. The demand for this valuable commodity created the need for cheap, strong labour, capable of withstanding the rigours of the Caribbean climate. And so was born the slave trade — and the interminable wars between Spain, France and England.

As a direct consequence of the Napoleonic Wars, beet sugar came to prominence as a source of sugar. Although the extraction had been developed previously by a German scientist, the technique was refined at the orders of Napoleon as a means of beating the English blockade of France and her shipping, thus ensuring a source of this precious foodstuff. Ever since that time, sugar beet has been increasing its share of the world's sugar market.

As the western world became more mechanised and richer, so the consumption of sugar rose until the annual consumption per head of population in some of the richest countries reached as much as 100 lbs (45 kg) in the early part of this century before levelling off and, indeed, falling in recent years.

'Sugar' is the common name given to one substance in daily use — *sucrose*. Sugars are chemical substances varying from quite simple to large complex molecules. All are *carbohydrates* or compounds composed of the elements carbon, hydrogen and oxygen. It is from the first two that their name is derived, in fact the French for Hydrate of Carbon (a very inaccurate term). Perhaps the best definition of a carbohydrate is that it is either a simple sugar or a compound made up of simple sugars joined together. The main sugars of interest to us as winemakers and brewers are *glucose* and *fructose*. The former is to be found as the product of *cane sugar* or *beet sugar*, as well as the compound that we require in our bodies to store and transport energy. The latter is found widely in nature in fruits and honey. *Starch,* another carbohydrate of importance, is to be found in grain and cereals, as well as plant tubers like potatoes.

These compounds form a vital part of our diet. From them is made available to our bodies either instant energy which we need for any activity; or stored in the muscles as glycogen, (a compound made up of thousands of glucose molecules), for future needs.

Carbohydrates are nature's source of energy. Nearly all life, whether plant or animal, depends on sugars in one form or another for energy to grow, breed, or, in the case of animals, move. They are also vital compounds used in the storing of energy. A potato, for example, is simply a store of starch for the plant's benefit to feed the plant during the sunless winter, and to provide a source of food for a developing young plant. We have discovered that the potato is an excellent source of cheap food and so make good use of it.

Although we require protein to build our bodies, vitamins to catalyse some of our metabolism, and fats to aid in digestion of certain vitamins (as well as for forming a store of fuel), we predominantly need carbohydrates to give us energy. Most of us at some time or another have taken a glucose tablet or sweet drink because we feel faint − in other words we are lacking in instant energy.

It is true to say that, apart from vitamins, proteins, and some fats, our diet is basically sugar or contains significant amounts of it. Starchy foods, as well as 'sweets', are well known as sources of sugars and reviled as such. Even healthy foods recommended for dieting, such as celery or carrots, have 1.5 and 5.5 gms of glucose in every 100 grams of the vegetable respectively.

Whatever the views held about the dangers or benefits of sugar, it is important to realise that nearly all our energy is derived from sugars. So, whatever is being said about the evils of sugar in our diets, we need a certain amount each day. Certainly as winemakers and brewers, we need at least some sugar in our *wort* or *must* before fermentation can take place.

To exclude completely sugar from your diet is, to say the least, counter productive; for sugar is the basic fuel of your body. It may not be utilised in the body in the form in which you eat it, but it is when split in half. The common, or household, sugar is *sucrose*. This is made up of two molecules of *glucose* joined together. It is glucose which the body requires to give it the energy for life. We may eat all sorts of 'pure' foodstuffs, but, at the end of the day, the sugar component is commonly glucose.

A simple example of the importance of sugar in the diet is that the diabetic will rapidly suffer serious complications of the disease if he or she over indulges in sugar. The insulin in the body cannot cope with the excess sugar and the patient may become *hyperglycaemic* (too much sugar in the blood). Conversely, a lack of sugar leads to *hypoglycaemia* or low blood sugar; a condition just as possibly fatal as the former. (See *Chapter 13.)*

There have been reports blaming sugar for most of the ills of mankind – from dental caries to death. Each report is supported by masses of scientific data. Conversely, the Sugar Council has produced data to prove that sugar is entirely harmless! There are papers by the hundreds both lauding and condemning 'sugar' in our diets. How on earth are we to make sense of such conflicting opinions?

The simple truth of the matter is that any substance in excess is dangerous. No-one in their right mind would try even a minute amount of what is known to be a poisonous substance. While sugar, so far from being poisonous is essential for life, it is still necessary to take a balanced view of the matter.

If you are overweight, you must cut down on your calories. If you take sugar in tea or coffee, it is a simple matter to reduce by a significant amount your daily calories by simply going without sugar – instead, if you must, use an artificial sweetener. To avoid obesity and the illnesses that can bring, it is obvious to restrict one's dietary intake to within the limits you know will avoid this 'middle age spread'. In addition, exercise will help with your general health.

The point that I am trying to make is that excess calorific intake will lead, inevitably, to obesity; it is this that can lead to heart disease, diabetes, arthritic diseases, and the rest of the catalogue of disasters laid at the door of sugar; although, to be entirely fair, there are the occasional medical conditions in which sugar has to be used with greater care.

So, quite simply, it makes sense to control your calorific intake at all stages of your day, and in all areas of your diet. This also includes alcohol. By choosing to drink dry wines in preference to sweet (or sweeten artificially), one's diet can be kept under strict control without any loss of pleasure in a drink, or having to go without something else in order to allow yourself a drink.

What is the place of sugar in winemaking and brewing? Do not forget that whatever people might say about 'sugar-free' wines or beers, these are, by definition, impossible for us to make. Without sugar to feed the yeast that conducts our fermentations, there can be no fermentation and, hence, no alcohol.

The other great 'free' subject today, is that of 'alcohol-free' wines and beers. Firstly, as we have seen, this is impossible for us to achieve. Secondly, none of these drinks are completely free of alcohol. They all contain less than 2% alcohol, and therefore, qualify as *'soft drinks'*; all of which are considered to be *'alcohol free'* based upon the legal definition of alcoholic beverages.

To be fair to the brewers, they have not only taken legal advice on this matter but have also chosen this name to try to be as unconfusing as possible. If some chose to call their products *'low alcohol'* it would help nobody but rather confuse the entire issue. Not only that, but the *'shandy'* sold in the corner shop would have to be renamed or redefined as a low alcohol product.

To summarise: we have seen that we need sugar not only in our daily diet in moderate amounts but also in fermentation. The aspects of health merely touched upon in this chapter will be dealt with in greater detail later.

3　Making a Sugar Free Wine

Let me make one thing quite clear. It is impossible to produce alcohol at home without the use of sugar. Yeast, which is added to the must (or mixture of ingredients from which is made a wine) or wort (the mixture of ingredients that make a beer), requires sugar to feed it. Without this it would either die or become dormant. Fermentation is, by definition, the transformation of sugars to alcohol by the action of yeast upon the sugar present. So, having said that we are making 'sugar free' wines, just what do we mean by this statement?

Sugar free, in winemaking terms, is the absence of detectable sugar *after fermentation has finished* – in other words a *dry wine* as tasted by the palate. Some people are unable to assess this accurately so methods of checking a wine for absence of sugar are required. Beers are more difficult to check because of the presence of dextrins.

One of the main aims of this book is to try to produce as 'natural' a wine as we can using, where possible, only natural ingredients and trying to avoid the use of what might be considered by some as 'chemicals'. We will certainly avoid those additives considered harmful.

Before we make a wine we need to gather some simple equipment together. All that you need at the outset are:

1　Two gallon bucket – with tight fitting lid of 'Food Grade'
1　Sieve
1　Wooden spoon

If you become serious in your winemaking, you will eventually require:

Demi-Johns
Bored stoppers (Rubber is a better material than cork)
Air-locks

Later still, you will need bottles and bottling equipment. But, for the present, this is all that you need.

Having collected the essentials, the next step is to look at the ingredients we shall need. For all wines we require the following ingredients:

Sugar
Acid
Tannin
Water
Nutrients

To which, of course, yeast has to be added to change the mixture into alcohol.

These ingredients are present in varying amounts in our base fruit or vegetable. Our object is to create a balance of the necessary ingredients to produce a good wine. Because the grape contains not only all these ingredients, but also contains them in the correct quantities and proportions, it has become, over the years, *the* wine making fruit. However, for those who do not have access to a vineyard, the main ingredients which provide the basic flavour to our homemade wines can be divided into the following groups:

Grape Concentrate
Pulp Fruit
Stone Fruit
Berry Fruit
Flower Petal
Leaf

Let us take a simple example to demonstrate how we can make an easy, pleasant wine with no problems attached, particularly for the beginner. With experience, the finished wine can be 'doctored' to vary the type of wine produced.

✷ Citrus Wine

Ingredient	Quantity per 2 gallon	Quantity per 10 litres
Orange juice	1 pint	500 mls
Grapefruit juice	1 pint	500 mls
Grape concentrate	½ pint	250 mls
Sugar	3½ lbs	1500 gms
Yeast	Sauternes	
Vitamin B$_1$	6 mg	6 mg
Water	to volume	to volume

For the recommended additives, see Page 53.

If you want to use honey instead of sugar you will need 3½ lbs per two gallons, or 1590 gms per litre. Before using this, it is necessary to heat it to ensure that it is sterile and then allow it to cool before adding to the must. Use any honey, but avoid some of the Australian blended ones which sometimes contain *Eucalyptus* pollen and can confer an unpleasant taste on a wine.

Method

After collecting the ingredients, prepare a yeast starter. Next, you must sterilise all equipment. First wash everything in hot water and then rinse it with sulphite solution. Do not inhale the gas this mixture gives off. As we shall see later, it can affect the lungs.

If you wish to avoid using this substance, you will need to sterilise all glass or metal equipment by heating it in the oven set at 150°C. Take care not to burn yourself — glass jars take a long time to cool down. Rubber, plastic or cork equipment cannot be sterilised this way since heat will either melt or otherwise destroy the corks or tubes. However, there is no better way to sterilise wine making equipment than by using sulphite. It is not toxic if not inhaled and can be guaranteed to destroy any harmful bacteria, although some people can be affected by its fumes. (See Chapter 12.)

Mix the ingredients, using about 1 lb of sugar and 5 pints of water. Sterilise with 100 ppm of sulphite (either 2 Campden tablets or the appropriate amount of stock solution) and, after 24 hours, add an active yeast starter. If you do not wish to use sulphite, use cooled boiled water, and add the active yeast starter immediately.

Every two or three days add another 10 ounces of sugar. In this way, the yeast will not be inhibited by large quantities of sugar, and the fermentation is less likely to 'stick' — or stop fermenting prematurely. When the fermentation dies down, make up to volume with cool, clean tap water.

The precise amount of sugar to add is determined by the gravity of the grape concentrate. Make sure that you measure it at the outset and check that you have got it right for the final volume of wine you are making. If you are using other sources of 'sugar', i.e. grape concentrate or juice, or honey, you will need to adjust the 'sugar additions' according to the specific gravity of your sugar.

As a rough rule of thumb:

1 lb Honey contains 14 oz sugar	(400 gms sugar/500 gms)
1 pint Grape Juice contains 4 oz sugar	(120 gms sugar/250 mls)
1 pint Grape Concentrate	
contains 1 lb sugar	(450 gms sugar/500 mls)
1 lb Raisins contain 10 oz sugar	(300 gms sugar/500 gms)

Check the acidity of the must which should be approximately 4 ppt. If it is too low, and this is unlikely, add either tartaric acid or lemon juice to bring the acidity up to the desired level. By keeping the acid level as low as this, the wine can be drunk while it is still young, and will make a pleasant aperitif, especially if the wine is dry.

To make a table wine, it will need longer maturing. This means that the acidity needs to be higher — about 5 ppt. The finished wine will probably need to be sweetened, unless you have a very dry palate. To do this, follow the guidelines in Chapter 5.

If you do not mind additives and you wish to lay the wine down, about 2 gms of Tannin per gallon is another variation that can be practiced with benefit to the wine. The tannin will make the wine a little more astringent and give it a bit more 'bite'. For diabetics the carbohydrate content of this wine is NIL, and the calorific content is approximately 70 calories per 100 mls.

Wines from Grape Concentrate

For the winemaker who does not wish to use 'additives', it is necessary to point out that grape concentrate may contain the following:

Ammonium Phosphate   Lactic Acid
Citric Acid   Saccharin
Flavourings   Sulphur Dioxide
Glucose Syrup   Tannin

An alternative ingredient is grape juice.

As we have said, we are aiming to produce a wine with an alcohol content of about 10%. In practical terms this means that the original gravity of our must needs to be about 70. Therefore, to take a typical commercial concentrate as an example, we find that the gravity will be about 350. In order to achieve our starting gravity it will need to be diluted to about five times its original volume.

Thus 1 pint of concentrate plus 4 pints of water will yield a must with this gravity.

i.e.   1 pint concentrate has SG of 350 dispersed in final volume
4 pints water have SG of 0 dispersed in final volume

Therefore, 5 pints of must has 350 units of specific gravity dispersed throughout its volume. If we divide 350 by 5 we get 70 — the SG of the must.

Working in litres, we will require:

900 mls Concentrate
3600 mls water

to produce a must with the same SG.

This working of the sum is convenient for this stated gravity of our concentrate since it means that this dilution yields 4.5 litres, the metric equivalent of one Imperial Gallon (4.5 litres).

If we use Imperial units we find that, to make one gallon (4.5 litres), we need:

1.6 pints of Concentrate (1 pint 12 oz)
6.4 pints of water (6 pints 8 oz)

However you 'do the sum', check it to make sure that you have not made a mistake. After making a yeast starter, sterilise your equipment. The next day make up the must as your calculations tell you, and pitch the yeast.

Check that the fermentation is complete by the methods outlined in Chapter 4, then rack and sulphite the wine (at the rate of 50 ppm) into a demi-john with a good stopper. Some winemakers prefer to use one of the proprietary types of safety corks but, with care and the checks detailed above, this should not be necessary.

Once the wine is mature (this usually means at least three months longer than the label says!) sweeten it, if you wish, using the method described in Chapter 5.

Winemakers' attitudes towards kit wines vary from the frankly disbelieving to the enthusiastic and prizewinning and, as with all things, the truth lies somewhere in between. The main advantages of these wines are the convenience of knowing that the finished product will be reasonably consistent time after time and that they take less time to make. On the other hand, many winemakers feel that to make 'home made wines' from such ingredients is cheating and simply 'will not do!'.

Such a wine will, if fermented to dryness, have about 70 calories per 100 mls. For the diabetic the carbohydrate content will be NIL.

So far I have only outlined two recipes for wines that are simple to make. Further recipes are suggested in each chapter. Outline methods are given in this chapter. In the chapter dealing with Diabetes, I shall include data about various ingredients; particularly their calorific and sugar contents.

In each 'medical' chapter, I have included the herbal aspects of that chapter. Apart from balancing any negative opinions about alcohol, the herbs listed are known to be of medicinal value in the conditions mentioned at that point of the book and either were, or still are, being used in herbal medicine. Indeed, some of the plants mentioned are in current use in 'proper' medicine even today. The index contains a complete list of recipes by fruit as well as by type of ingredient as listed above.

Where the recipe states 'sugar', this can be taken to mean whichever form of additional sugar you prefer — household, honey, grape concentrate, or grape juice. Of course it is possible to experiment and use a proportion of two or more of these sugars.

Pulp Fermentation

Apple Wine

For the average winemaker, the making of apple wine entails the use of pulp fermentation. However, should you possess a fruit juicer, the job of preparing the ingredients is that much easier.

Method I – Using additives.   If you do not have a juicer, the problem is to estimate the natural sugar content of the fruit. As a rule of thumb, apples can be assumed to contain about 2 oz of natural sugar per pound of fruit. Obviously, a juice extraction will take the guesswork out of this and, if you can use a juicer, do so. Otherwise, it is necessary to chop up the apples, removing any damaged parts. Place them in a sterilised bucket containing 3 pints of water to which one Campden Tablet has been added. Add the nutrients and pectic enzyme.

✳ Apple Wine

Ingredient	Quantity per gallon	Quantity per 5 litres
Apples	6 lbs	3 kgs
Sugar	to SG 70	to SG 70
Yeast		
Vitamin B_1	6 mg	6 mg
Water	to volume	to volume

For the recommended additives, see Page 53.

If you prepare a yeast starter at the same time as the apples, the starter will be fully active by the time the sulphite level has fallen to a level which will not inhibit the yeast.

If you are not practicing *exponential feeding,* add the permitted amount of sugar – See Table 12 – after calculating the natural sugar content. Either allow 2 oz per pound of fruit used, or, if you have used a juicer, measure the SG of the juice extracted.

When the fermentation has died down, make to volume. Ferment to dryness.

Apples often contain a compound called *Sorbitol*. Because of this, an apple wine often tastes medium dry and not dry as expected, when young. Tests for residual sugar are not affected by this, nor is the carbohydrate content affected for the diabetic.

If juice extraction was used, the method is as for any wine: sugar additions, and general supervision of fermentation.

If pulp fermentation is used, however, the carbon dioxide given off once the fermentation becomes established will raise up the fruit in the must so that it forms a *cap*. This can lead to infection if it is not broken up and stirred into the must twice a day.

Do not allow pulp fermentation to continue longer than four days or the wine will be rough and bitter due to excess acid and tannin entering the wine from the fruit as fermentation continues.

After this time, strain the fruit from the must and press the pulp — lightly. Do not try to wring out the last drop as this can lead to a haze in the finished wine. Now the final sugar can be added — either in stages if using exponential feeding, or in 'one go' if not. Make to volume, and continue fermentation under air lock.

Once fermentation has finished, by whichever method the wine is made, it has to be racked and sulphited at the rate of 100 ppm (or two Campden Tablets). Maturation is now carried out in the usual way. Sweetening can be done, if desired by using the method given in Chapter 5.

This method can be used for the following fruit:

Pears — using 3 lbs of fruit per gallon (1500 gms/5l)
Crab Apple — using 2-3 lbs per
   gallon   (1000-1500 gms/5l)
Quince — using 3 lbs per gallon   (1500 gms/5l)

Method II — using no additives.   Beware! If you decide not to use additives, you must not use a steam juice extractor because of the pectin this will release. To reduce the oxidative browning that will occur, use lemon juice in place of sulphite, about 10-15 mls of juice in the water.

To minimise oxidation and infection, it is vital to prepare a yeast starter before beginning to prepare the ingredients so that it can be pitched as soon as the must is prepared. Mix the fruit, juice or pulp, malt extract, and some of the sugar, and pitch the yeast.

From this point the method is identical as *Method I* — with the exception of sulphite. Because of the sterilising actions of this compound, not using it makes it imperative to ensure that all equipment is scrupulously clean and sterilised by heat before use. Take every precaution to prevent bacteria entering the wine at all stages of production.

Not using sulphite reduces the shelf life of a wine, unless it is pasteurised. This is a specialist technique involving heating the wine to 140°F (60°C) for 3 minutes. If used at home, take great care not to heat sealed bottles — they can explode from pressure inside when heated, or implode from lowered pressure as they are cooled. 'Over-cooking' a wine will ruin its taste. So, this is not a method recommended for the amateur. Rather, take great care in avoiding infection.

Comparing the two methods highlights the differences between them. The only real alteration in production technique is in the use, or not, of 'additives'. As I have said, if you are not using sulphite take extra care over the prevention of infection and oxidation.

Rhubarb Wine

Contrary to popular belief, rhubarb is not a poisonous fruit. Page upon page in amateur winemaking books describe how to reduce the 'dangerous' acidity of rhubarb by the use of precipitated chalk; and then how to replace it with various mixtures. This is all based on the erroneous belief that the fruit stalks of the plant contain significant amounts of poisonous *oxalic acid*. This is wrong.

The leaves most certainly do contain large amounts of this acid, and there were several cases of oxalic acid causing death due to poisoning when the leaves were cooked and eaten in mistake for spinach.

As a matter of fact, both spinach and strawberries contain more oxalic acid than rhubarb! So, it can be seen that the small amount present in the stalks of rhubarb is not harmful. Having said that, it is important to realise that some people are sensitive to even the minutest amount of this acid. The subject of allergy is discussed in Chapter 9.

If you are one of those unfortunate people who are upset by oxalic acid — manifest usually by indigestion or stomach upset after eating the fruit or drinking the wine — it is wise to presume sensitivity and therefore abstain from either eating or drinking it.

✳ **Rhubarb Wine**

Ingredient	Quantity per gallon	Quantity per 5 litres
Rhubarb	4 lbs	2 kg
Sugar	to SG 70	to SG 70
Hock yeast		
Vitamin B_1	6 mg	6 mg
Water	to volume	to volume
Tannin	¼ teaspoon	

For the recommended additives, see Page 53.

Wash the fruit carefully. Remove any damaged parts before chopping the fruit stalks into short lengths, and then slice them into three lengthwise. Add three pints of cold water. Under no circumstances use hot water because oxalic acid is more soluble with heat. By using a cold extraction method the amount of the acid entering the must is minimised.

If desired, add sulphite to sterilise the must and, after 24 hours add an active yeast starter, together with the nutrients and sugar; otherwise add the starter and other ingredients. When fermentation has died down, make to volume. Ferment to dryness under air lock.

Keep a close watch on the maturing wine in case a *malolactic* fermentation occurs. This ingredient is said to be especially likely to undergo this 'reaction', which is, in fact, infection by *lactobacilli*. It is quite harmless, but may cause bottles to explode! After the usual fermentation steps, sweeten to taste.

One variation which can be tried is to emulate a light *Hock-type* wine by the addition of either elderflower petals (2 oz per gallon; or 60 gms per 5 litres) or rose petals ($\frac{1}{2}$ pint per gallon, or 250 mls per 5 litres). Both of these additions are when using *fresh* flowers. If you are using dried flowers, use a maximum of $\frac{1}{2}$ oz (15 gms) and $\frac{1}{5}$ oz (6 gms) respectively.

These are added after the first violent fermentation has died down. If added too soon, the esters which give the wine its bouquet, will be driven off by the large amounts of carbon dioxide produced in the early part of fermentation. To avoid the need to strain the wine, it is a good idea to suspend the flowers in the wine in a muslin or nylon bag. If you use rose petals, be certain to use a white species — there are no rosé hocks!

Stone Fruit for White Wine

Peach Wine

One of the more popular homemade winemaking ingredients is peach. It can be used to make one of the best wines in amateur circles.

★ Peach Wine

Ingredients	Quantity per 2 gallon	Quantity per 10 litres
Peaches	3 lbs	1500 gms
Sugar	to SG 70	to SG 70
Yeast	Sherry or Tokay	
Tannin	$\frac{1}{4}$ teaspoon	1 gm
Tartaric acid	$\frac{1}{3}$ oz	10 gms
Pectic enzyme		
Water	to volume	to volume

For the recommended additives, see Page 53.

Wipe the peaches with a clean muslin cloth. After stoning the fruit, pulp, and sterilise with sulphite if desired. Strain through a muslin or nylon cloth to remove the fruit pulp. Press lightly.

21

Peach and apricot stones can contain small amounts of *cyanide* — a highly poisonous substance. Hence, to avoid this compound getting into a wine, the fruit should be stoned. But, it must be emphasised, the risks are minute.

Add the nutrients and an active yeast starter. Add the permitted sugar in stages. When fermentation has died down, make to volume. Ferment to dryness under air lock, and rack before maturing in the usual manner. Sweeten to taste as described in Chapter 5.

This method can be used for the following fruit:

Apricot — using 3 lbs fruit per gallon (1500 gms/5l)
Dried Apricot — using 1 lb per gallon (500 gms/5l)
Dried Peaches — using 1 lb per gallon (500 gms/5l)

Stone Fruit for Red Wine

Unlike the fruit mentioned in the last section, red fruit do not require stoning before fermentation.

★ Plum Wine

Ingredient	Quantity per gallon	Quantity per 5 litres
Plums	3 lbs	1500 gms
Sugar	to SG 70	to SG 70
Pommard yeast		
Vitamin B$_1$	3 mg	3 mg
Pectic enzyme		
Water	to volume	to volume

For the recommended additives, see Page 53.

Crush the fruit. Pour two or three pints of boiling water over them. This has the advantage of not only sterilising the fruit, but also aiding colour extraction. This will increase the pectin content and so make the use of pectic enzyme more important in order to avoid a haze in the finished wine. *Allow to cool.*

Next, add the pectic enzyme. If you add this before the temperature of the must has dropped below 80°F (26°C), the heat will denature the enzyme rendering it inactive so that it cannot work on the fruit to break down their fibres to help in extraction of the colour and destruction of the pectin.

Add the nutrients and an active yeast starter at the same time, together with the sugar.

Ferment on the pulp for three or four days before straining. Do not forget to break up the cap of fruit twice or three times each day. This not only aids colour and flavour extraction but also minimises the risks of infection.

When fermentation has died down, make to volume. Ferment to dryness under air lock in the usual way before racking and maturing for 9-12 months. Sweeten to taste as described in Chapter 5.

This method can be used for the following fruit:

Damson — using 3 lbs fruit per gallon   (1500 gms/5l)
Cherry — using 4 lbs fruit per gallon   (2000 kgs/5l)

Berries for White Wine

✳ Gooseberry Wine

Ingredient	Quantity per 2 gallons	Quantity per 10 litres
Gooseberries	4 lbs	2 kgs
Sugar	to SG 70	to SG 70
Bordeaux yeast		
Tartaric acid	$\frac{1}{3}$ oz	10 gms
Vitamin B$_1$	6 mg	6 mg
Pectic enzyme		
Water	to volume	to volume

For the recommended additives, see Page 53.

Crush the fruit and cover with water. Add pectic enzyme and sulphite in order to sterilise the fruit. After 24 hours, add sugar, nutrients, and an active yeast starter.

If you choose not to use sulphite, use boiling water to sterilise the fruit before crushing. Allow to cool and then proceed without the sulphite.

Ferment on the pulp for four days, strain and top up to the final volume. Ferment to dryness under air lock.

Mature for at least one year after final racking. Sweeten to taste as described in Chapter 5.

As a variation on the recipe, a light *Moselle* type wine can be made using *Elderflower*. Between $\frac{1}{4}$ and $\frac{1}{2}$ pint of fresh flowers are added at the beginning of fermentation, using a *Hock* yeast. Remove the flowers at the same time as the fruit, and proceed with fermentation and maturation as with the basic wine.

Berries for Red Wine

Elderberry

Much has been written about the superiority of this fruit for winemaking. It is even said to have been added to *Port* to improve its quality in poor years! If this is true, it is obviously the parent of a superb wine when properly made.

The amount of this fruit used in wines varies considerably, depending on the type of wine being made.

If making a high alcohol table wine, or fortified wine, (such as a port type wine), 4 lbs or more per gallon are required.

However, when making a lighter bodied wine with a lower alcohol strength, the fruit should be limited to 2 lbs per gallon.

Remove the berries from their stalks. The inclusion of any of the *strigs* will make the wine bitter. Crush the berries and cover with boiling water to sterilise the fruit. After cooling, add the nutrients, pectic enzyme, and an active yeast starter.

Pulp ferment for three or four days. More will make the wine too astringent (too high in tannin). It is better to have a lighter coloured wine with the correct tannin than a wine of a deep red colour which is too low in alcohol and thin-bodied for its high tannin content.

When fermentation has died down, make to volume. Ferment to dryness under air lock. Mature for at least one year. Sweeten to taste, as outlined in Chapter 5. However, most wines of this type are usually better dry.

This method can be used for the following fruit:

Bilberry — using 2 lbs fruit per gallon (1000 gms/5l)
Dried Elderberry — using ½ lb fruit per
   gallon (500 gms/5l)
Dried Bilberry — using ½ lb fruit per gallon (500 gms/5l)

✱ Elderberry Wine

Ingredient	Quantity per gallon	Quantity per 1 litre
Elderberries	2 lbs	1 kgm
Sugar	SG 70	SG 70
Acid		to acidity 4.5
Pommard yeast		
Pectic enzyme		
Vitamin B_1	6 mg	6 mg
Water	to volume	to volume

For the recommended additives, see Page 53.

Elderflower Wine

If this wine is allowed to mature for long enough, it is one of the pleasantest 'country wines' there are. It will usually be reaching its peak when the next year's flowers are ready for gathering. So, make it this year and drink it next year.

Take care to collect the flowers on a dry day. Always sniff the flowers before picking them to make sure that they do not have that characteristic 'catty' smell about them. A wine made from such flowers may often be ruined by a poor or inappropriate bouquet.

Flower wines are particularly deficient in acid and nutrients. The basic ingredient can be said to be totally lacking in sugar. Thus, strictly speaking, we are making a sugar wine with a flavouring — in this case of elderflowers.

No more than 1 pint of flowers is needed per gallon of wine. When picking make sure that it is only the white — and not the creamy coloured — florets that you take.

Do not forget that it is now illegal to pick any wild plants on common ground. You may only do so on private ground with the owner's permission.

✱ Elderflower Wine

Ingredient	Quantity per 2 gallons	Quantity per 10 litres
Elderflowers	1 pint	500 mls
Raisins	½ lb	250 gms
or		
Grape concentrate	½ pint	250 mls
Pectic enzyme		
Sauterne yeast		
Vitamin B$_1$	12 mg	12 mg
Water	to volume	to volume
Citric acid		
Malic acid	mixed to acidity 4.5	
Tartaric acid		
Tannin	⅐ oz	4 gms
or		
Tea		
Glycerine	1 teaspoon	5 mls

For the recommended additives, see Page 53.

Remove the petals from their stalks, ensuring that there are no 'green bits' remaining. If present they will impart a bitter flavour to the wine.

Mix all the ingredients together, making sure that the sugar and grape concentrate are fully mixed together.

If using raisins, instead of grape concentrate, first wash and then chop raisins. Place them in a pan with 2 pints of boiling water and simmer gently for twenty minutes. Before adding this mixture to the other ingredients, make certain that it has cooled to 70°F, (21°C) − or thereabouts. The raisins are pulp fermented with the flowers.

Either sterilise with sulphite at the rate of 50 ppm, and after 24 hours add an active yeast starter; or add the active yeast starter as soon as cool enough. Ferment on the pulp for four to five days, and then strain into gallon jars with air locks and make to volume.

Ferment to dryness. When fermentation is complete, rack and sulphite prior to maturing under cork.

Sweeten to taste as described in Chapter 5.

Glycerine is a most useful additive to this wine as it gives the wine a pleasant smoothness, and imparts a slight sweetness.

4 Testing Sugar Free Wine and Beer

Throughout this book, the importance of fermenting to dryness is emphasised. Not only is this of benefit in general dietary terms but, for the diabetic, it is imperative. This ensures accurate control in the diabetic's diet of both carbohydrate and calories and above all, it ensures no residual sugar in the wine.

TABLE 1

Tests to do on all Wines

Test	How Performed	Purpose	Range of Readings
Specific Gravity	Hydrometer	(a) Sugar Assay (b) Potential Alcohol (c) Progress of Fermentation	(a) No more than 30 oz/gal (190 gm/litre). SG no more than 1070 (b) Not to exceed 10%
Original Gravity	S.G. of Natural sugar+Added Sugar	Specific Gravity of total sugar	Not to exceed 1070
Final Gravity	S.G. at end of Fermentation	To ensure a DRY wine	Less than 1000 See Table 13 p. 139
Temperature Correction	Measure Temp of test solution	To ensure accurate S.G.	See Table 2 for Corrections
Residual Sugar	S.G. checked by Clinitest	To ensure a DRY wine	S.G. less than 1000 Clinitest $<\frac{1}{2}\%$
Calorific Content	See Page 38		
Carbohydrate Content	See Chapter 9		

Table 1 continued

Tests to do on all Wines

Test	How Performed	Purpose	Range of Readings
Alcohol Content	See Page 37		
Pectin	Methyl Alcohol	To exclude as cause of Haze	See Chapter 4.
Starch	Iodine		
Acidity	Titration	Benefit to: (a) taste (b) keeping (c) antisepsis	Depends on wine type and palate See Page 34-36

After making your wine, carry out the listed tests. For the diabetic, *these are essential,* as discussed in the chapter on diabetes.

If you wish a sweet wine, we shall see in Chapter 5 how to achieve this.

Testing for sugar.   As we will see, in Chapter 13, residual sugar must be forbidden in any diabetic drink, whether alcoholic or not.

Methods of measuring sugar content are:

(1) Specific Gravity
(2) Clinitest
(3) Clinistix, Diastix, or Diabur 5000
(4) Fehling's Solution
(5) Benedict's Solution

The last two involve boiling strong caustic solutions and thus are not recommended for the amateur.

After preparing the must, strain it if necessary. Then measure the specific gravity. Make the appropriate correction for temperature, and deduct a figure of 7. This arbitrary number is a 'guesstimate' of the amount the solids in the must contribute to the SG.

Measuring Specific gravity, we can gain some idea of:
Sugar content
Total sugar content

Residual sugar *(roughly)*
Potential alcohol content
Progress of fermentation

The sugar and total sugar contents can be read from Table 14 as can the approximate potential alcohol content.

The sugar content is only unknown in the original juice. After measuring this and estimating the natural sugar in the recipe, try to be precise in your measurement of further sugar additions so that the total sugar content is known reasonably accurately.

The reading for potential alcohol content obtained from specific gravity readings is not a very accurate figure — except under optimum conditions. It is, however, a useful guide to the strength that the finished wine will have.

While it is possible to monitor the progress of fermentation by serial specific gravity readings, it is a possible way of introducing infection into the wine. So it is probably better, especially if you do not use sulphite in your winemaking, to avoid opening the jar too often.

When you are certain that fermentation has finished, take another reading of the specific gravity. The signs that indicate the end of fermentation are the cessation of bubbles passing through the air lock and the water level the same on both sides of the lock.

Unfortunately, it is not enough to say that a specific gravity below 1000 means that fermentation is complete. Depending on the starting gravity, the final gravity varies. So, before assuming that fermentation has finished, check what the final gravity should be from Table 14. If this is correct (again, do not forget the temperature correction), then the wine or beer may be racked to start its maturation.

The hydrometer is one of the wine and beer maker's basic pieces of equipment, particularly when precise control of fermentation and alcohol content is required. While there is a place for science in winemaking and brewing, the old, true and tried methods that are easy to use form the backbone of testing at home. It is later, when fermentation is complete, that we may need the more scientific tests.

Using the Hydrometer

Many winemakers and brewers seem to have problems in

using a hydrometer. In fact, this is a most useful and easy to use 'tool'.

A hydrometer is usually made of glass, thin at one end and bulbous at the other. Before using one, examine it. Along the length of the thin upper end is marked a scale, below which is to be found a temperature — for example 60°F. This refers to the temperature at which the readings obtained are accurate.

As well as the hydrometer itself, you will need a 'Trial Jar'. Although these are obtainable as such, in practice any thin tall clear glass or plastic container will do — a milk bottle for example — provided, of course, it is scrupulously clean.

TABLE 2

Corrections to Hydrometer
Readings at Various Temperatures

Temperature °F	Correction to last figure of reading
50	Subtract 0.6
59	CORRECT
68	Add 0.9
77	Add 2.0
86	Add 3.4
95	Add 5.0
104	Add 6.8

After the normal sterilising of the equipment, take a sample of the wine or beer to be tested and place it in the trial jar. Carefully lower the hydrometer into the jar. When it stops bobbing up and down, look along the fluid level to see the number on the scale to which the hydrometer has sunk. This figure is the Specific Gravity of the test fluid. Most likely, the hydrometer will be calibrated from 980 to 1200. These figures refer to the ratio of the density of the test liquid to that of pure water. The figures used in winemaking and brewing vary; typically, we hear of 20, 1020, or 1.020. All these numbers mean the same thing. The specific gravity of water can be taken as 0, or 1000, or 1. What we therefore have, is a scale which tells us how much more or less than water the Specific Gravity of our wine or beer is.

From using the hydrometer, we can gauge several facts about a wine or beer. Table 1 gives a list of tests to do on a wine; included are several which rely on the hydrometer.

Sugar Measurement

Once the hydrometer confirms that the fermentation is finished, the chemical methods of assay can be called into play.

There are two groups of these tests. First, the older methods which involve boiling are not recommended for home use. The more modern tests use either 'dipsticks' or tablets. In fact, they are the older tests put into convenient packages.

The best known test is that used daily by millions of diabetics the world over. This is, of course, *Clinitest*. The test 'reagent' is a tablet composed of copper sulphate, mixed with citric acid, sodium carbonate and sodium hydroxide.

The acid is to ensure that the pH is correct for the chemical reaction that is to take place. Sodium carbonate 'fizzes' when wetted — thus, the 'ingredients' are well mixed in the solution; while the sodium hydroxide is for actually making the reaction occur.

When wetted, the tablets dissolve and effervesce to ensure mixing of the solution formed. At the same time the solution becomes very hot. In order to avoid burning yourself, always place the test tube in the rack provided. The heat is essential for the reaction to take place.

Before using *Clinitest*, always make sure that the test tube is absolutely clean. It must be placed upright in its rack. To perform the test, place 5 drops of wine and 10 drops of sterile water in the test tube. Shake the tube gently to mix them, and then add one *Clinitest* tablet to the mixture. As the tube fizzes, it heats up and during the reaction that is taking place, carbon dioxide is given off. More importantly, there is a colour change.

What happens is that copper oxide is formed in the presence of glucose. Depending on the amount of glucose present, this oxide takes on different colours. For those interested, the reaction is:

$$2CuSO_4 \; + \; 4NaOH \; \rightarrow \; Cu_2O \; + \; 2Na_2SO_4 \; + \; H_2O$$

Copper Sulphate	+	Sodium Hydroxide	->	Copper Oxide	+	Sodium Sulphate	+ Water

Once the boiling has stopped, wait for 15 seconds, gently shake the tube again, and then compare the colour in the tube with the colour chart provided with the kit.

There are, however, some drawbacks to the use of *Clinitest*. It does not only measure the presence, and the amount, of glucose; it also detects any reducing substance. Among a list of such compounds are aldehydes, salicylic acid (aspirin), glucose, fructose, and ascorbic acid. These all contain a chemical group called a carbonyl group which reacts with the copper to form different colours, depending on which substance is present.

For the wine or beer maker, those that matter are the sugars fructose and glucose, to which we also have to add ascorbic acid or *Vitamin C*. This vitamin is present in many fresh fruits and vegetables. However, it will disappear during fermentation because every five days the amount of vitamin C will halve. Thus, if we consider blackcurrants which contain 200 mgm ascorbic acid in every 100 gms, a must containing 3 lbs per gallon (1.5 kg per 5 litres), will have nearly 4.5 gms in the must. If the fermentation period is taken to be five weeks; the level of the vitamin will have fallen to 35 mgs per 100 mls. This is too small to affect the *Clinitest* test.

So, if you wish to use ascorbic acid as an antioxidant, instead of sulphite, do not add it until after performing the *Clinitest* test. Do not forget that it is an acid and will, therefore, raise the acidity of the wine.

Because *Clinitest* was not developed for use by winemakers, the system is not calibrated to our use. Before using it, it is necessary to do a series of experiments to find out the readings you will get with different wines.

Take a wine that is absolutely dry. Test it as described above. The reading obtained will give the colour for a dry wine. Do this on wines that are both white and red.

Next make solutions of the wine containing rising amounts of sugar, in accordance with the range of the test — from $\frac{1}{4}$% to 2%. Test each sample and make a note of the colour obtained. This may not correspond with the colour chart with the kit. This is, as stated above, due to other compounds affecting the test. It is of no importance. What matters is the colours obtained using wines.

In practice, the only readings we are concerned with are 0%, $\frac{1}{4}$% and $\frac{1}{2}$%. Above this, the wine cannot be said to be free of residual sugar.

If you wish to be thorough, it is worth considering a series of solutions to test. These should include:

1. Water.
2. Weak household sugar (less than 2%).
3. Weak invert sugar. To produce this, boil household sugar in water solution with citric acid.
4. A variety of wines of differing sweetness.

Perform the test on each sample. The results should be as follows:

1. Negative. There should be no reducing substances in water.
2. Negative. Household sugar is not a reducing agent, and, therefore, is not detectable by *Clinitest.*
3. Variable. Depending on the strength of the solution, and the colour chart you prepared earlier.
4. Variable. Depending on the sweetness or dryness of the wines being tested.

Household sugar is inverted by yeasts. So, unless you have just added extra sugar to a non-fermenting wine, a negative test can be assumed accurate.

There are several dipstick methods for testing for glucose: *Clinistix, Diastix,* and *Diabur 5000.* They are specific for glucose but, as their accuracy depends on a large number of factors such as temperature and pH, they are not recommended. A comparatively large volume of wine is needed for these tests — which is another reason for not using them.

Testing Acidity

Acidity plays an important rôle in many aspects of winemaking as, indeed, it does in the finished wine.

To measure the amount of free acid in either the must or the wine, take 10 mls of the test solution and place it in a conical flask. If you are testing the must, it may require filtration before testing to remove suspended solids. A wine, as long as it is reasonably clear, will not need filtration.

If the wine is white, dilute the sample with 30-40 mls of distilled water. Red wines or their musts will need to be diluted to

300-400 mls, again with distilled water, in order to dilute the colour sufficiently to be able to see the 'end point' of the reaction.

To this diluted sample, add 2 or 3 drops of phenolphthalein. This substance is what is known as an *indicator,* and has the property of changing colour at an almost neutral pH. Thus, it is possible to measure the amount of alkali needed to neutralise the acid in the solution.

Next, place deci-normal, (one-tenth strength), *Sodium Hydroxide* in a burette. Make a note of the level that the solution reaches. This is added, half a millilitre at a time, to the flask containing the wine. As it is added, the test sample becomes red at the point where the wine and alkali mix. At first, this is transient; but, as the 'end point' is reached, (the point at which the colour change is permanent), the colour fades more slowly, until the end point is reached. It is now that the colour becomes permanent. As the end point is neared, add the alkali more slowly, until the addition of one more drop produces the final change.

The final colour is the merest hint of a cherry-red in a white wine, and a smokey-grey in a red wine.

The volume of alkali that was added is now read from the burette. To do this, subtract the final reading of the level of the alkali in the burette from the original. This gives the total volume of sodium hydroxide required.

From this figure, the amount of acid, measured in parts of acid per thousand parts of wine *(ppt),* is obtained by dividing the volume of alkali used by two.

This figure is the amount of acid in the wine, expressed as though all the acid were *sulphuric acid.* Although this acid is not used in winemaking or brewing, and is not present in wine or beer, it is a convenient unit of measurement. (It is possible to express the acidity in ppt of other acids, but, in practice, sulphuric acid is used as the unit.) Having measured the acidity, it may now need to be adjusted.

Do not forget when assaying the acidity of a must that the reading may have been made upon a volume *less* than the final planned volume. To correct the reading of an Imperial measure, divide the reading by 8, and then multiply this by the volume of tested juice in pints. This simple calculation will give you the acidity of one gallon of the must — measured in ppt.

For example, if 6 pints of must have an acidity of 8, this will give a final acidity of 6 ppt in one gallon of must, or 3 ppt in two gallons of must:

$$\frac{6 \text{ pints} \times 8 \text{ ppt}}{8 \text{ pints}} = 6 \text{ ppt for 1 gal; or } \frac{6 \times 8}{16} \text{ 3 ppt for 2 gals}$$

If the acidity is too high, it will need to be reduced. For most home made wines this entails diluting the must to an appropriate level.

Should the acidity need raising, this can be done by using the wine acids. Opinion varies: some use one acid, others a mixture. For those who wish to avoid 'additives' the use of lemon juice will be more than adequate. However, it is more difficult to measure the increase of acidity using juice when compared with using acid. For example, 7 gms ($^1/_4$ oz) of tartaric acid will raise the acidity of one gallon of must by just over 1 ppt. On the other hand, it will be necessary to add some juice and repeat the test. Continue the process until the must has the correct acidity for the type of wine being made.

The range of acidities of various wine types is given in Table 3. These are the ranges suggested for wines intended for almost immediate consumption. If a wine is going to be matured for long periods, an acidity of 1-2 ppt greater than the table is suggested.

TABLE 3

Suggested Range of Acidity for Different Wine Types

Red Table Dry	4.0-6.0
Red Dessert	4.0-6.0
Rosé	5.0-7.0
White Dry	3.5-5.5
White Medium	4.0-6.0
White Sweet	4.5-6.5
White Sparkling	4.5-6.5
Sherry	3.0-5.5

Alcohol Content

The alcohol content, as already stated, is going to be limited to 10%. The reasons for this are discussed in earlier Chapters.

Achieving this goal is predominantly by controlling the Original Gravity and careful measurement of sugar additions. Be careful to include all fermentable sugar in the recipe; including the sugar in the fruit, grape concentrate, malt extract, as well as household sugar or honey added to raise the gravity to its permitted limit.

By adding up all the sugar in the must the *Potential Alcohol* content can be estimated. This is only an approximate calculation, but it does give some idea of the strength of the wine or beer.

A more accurate method of alcohol measurement involves boiling 100 mls of wine and an equal volume of distilled water. Measure these quantities carefully, place in a trial jar and take the specific gravity of this mixture. Do not forget to check the temperature and make the necessary corrections.

Transfer the mixture to a flask capable of withstanding heat and carefully boil the mixture. A few small pieces of clean gravel in the bottom of the flask will help stop the mixture boiling over or 'bumping'. Do not boil vigorously or you will lose other substances as well as water and alcohol.

When the solution is reduced to about one half of its original volume, remove from the heat and allow to cool to the temperature at which the first reading was taken. Do not try to cool too quickly or the glass flask may crack or worse.

Once cool, add distilled water to make the volume 200 mls again. Check the temperature of the solution and measure the specific gravity again.

This will be found to have risen. Because alcohol is lighter than water, a dry wine should have a final gravity less than that of water, ie less than 1000. So, remove the alcohol and replace it with water and the gravity will rise. From the increase in gravity, we can calculate the alcohol content of a wine.

The limits we have imposed on our wines, mean that the maximum increase in specific gravity allowed is 13. Table 4 gives the alcohol content of wines calculated from different gravity increases.

TABLE 4

Alcohol Content Measured by Boiling Method

Rise in S.G.	Alcohol Content	Rise in S.G.	Alcohol Content
1	0.66	14	10.51
2	1.34	15	11.40
3	2.02	16	12.30
4	2.71	17	13.20
5	3.42	18	14.10
6	4.14	19	15.10
7	4.88	20	16.00
8	5.63	21	17.00
9	6.40	22	18.00
10	7.18	23	19.00
11	7.98	24	20.00
12	8.80	25	21.00
13	9.65	26	22.00

From this it is clear that, if the gravity increase is kept to no more than 13, the finished wine will be well within our health limits of 10%.

Calorific Content

For most winemakers and brewers, the calorific content of your drinks is not that important. However, for the diabetic it is, despite the *Diabetic Association* considering only the carbohydrate content of foodstuffs. While it is essential to control the carbohydrate intake, there is little point in ignoring all sources of what may be excess calories. Do not forget that a diabetic has to watch not only the 'sugar' he or she eats, but also keep the weight under strict control.

To estimate the calorific value of a wine or beer is easy. Having calculated the total sugar content of the must or wort, work out how much is in 100 mls. Multiplying this figure by 7 will give a rough and ready guide to how fattening your drinks are.

While not entircly accurate – it in fact overestimates the calories – it is better to be above rather than below the true figure.

Another important consideration for the diabetic is the presence of any residual sugar in the wine or beer. If a wine is allowed to ferment to completion, there will be no residual sugar in the wine and hence, for the diabetic, the wine will have no carbohydrate content.

On the other hand, beer will always contain some carbohydrate because beers require dextrins for body and condition. Therefore, broadly speaking, they will always contain at least 2 gms of carbohydrate per ½ pint – even in the so called *Diabetic* beers that are available on the commercial market.

There is a paradox between calorific and carbohydrate content of drinks. If you examine the assay of some of the commercial diabetic drinks, you will see that they nearly all have carbohydrate contents of 2 gms per ½ pint. The calorific content, on the other hand, is frequently in excess of 100 calories per ½ pint.

By contrast, the commercial 'ordinary' beers also contain the same 100 calories, but about 10 gms of carbohydrate per ½ pint. As a result of this, many people will drink a DIÄT drink thinking to diet. Instead, to their amazement, they put on weight. And this misconception is by no means exclusive to diabetics!

Testing for Hazes

If a wine is not completely clear it is said to have a haze. The causes of this problem are many and varied. Most are preventable by the use of the correct equipment, ingredients, and care in the making of the wine.

Metal Hazes

To begin with the completely avoidable. Metal, if allowed into contact with an acid solution such as wine, will partially dissolve, causing a haze.

Some metals, such as lead, are extremely toxic. It is not a rapidly acting poison but builds up gradually in the body causing brain damage. Often the first sign of lead poisoning is a blue line along the gum margins in the mouth.

As far as home winemaking is concerned, lead is mostly seen in the old *soft glazed* pots and jars beloved of the 'old fashioned' winemaker. Their occurrence is increasingly rare, but the warning is, nonetheless, timely. Such jars are easily tested. A thumb nail will indent the solf lead glaze. Modern hard glazes are not marked.

Brewers do, it is true, use metal but the wort, at the boiling stage, is not acid enough to get the metal of the saucepan into solution. Some commercial breweries still use copper for their boiling vats. If it were winemaking, the copper would be dissolved, causing a haze.

Other metals which can get into a wine are iron, and zinc. The former is commonly introduced into the must when using a cracked or chipped enamel pan. Such an iron haze will be either white or bluish tinged.

To test for iron, add a few drops of sulphite solution. If a yellow precipitate develops, iron is possibly present. Alternatively, add hydrogen peroxide to a sample of the suspect wine or must. If the solution becomes turbid or cloudy within twenty four hours, it is more than probable that the wine will develop an iron haze.

To remove an iron haze, use either 5% tannic acid solution, or 5% citric acid in 10% sulphite solution. Before treating the bulk of the wine, do a trial on a small portion of the wine. Firstly, to see if the treatment will clear the wine, and secondly, to find out just how much solution is needed to remove the haze.

Zinc is also a toxic metal. It is used in the making of galvanised iron containers. The zinc, which is used to coat the iron, forms carbonate salts when it comes into contact with atmospheric carbon dioxide. These carbonate salts are soluble in acid solution. Thus, a must or wine placed in a galvanised zinc bucket will be guaranteed to have some zinc in it. Not only will this cause a haze but, more importantly, also add a toxic metal (the zinc) to your wine. Thus, avoid the use of zinc in winemaking.

Copper is not a toxic metal, but it can cause troubles in wine. In brewing, however, it poses no problem. Copper may be suspected of causing a problem if the wine shows a reddish haze or deposit. This is usually due to copper sulphide — formed by a reaction between the copper and sulphite. If present, it is not removable by the amateur, since the treatment involves the use of the even more poisonous ferro-cyanide.

It may be possible, if you wish to try it, to use casein to remove some of a metal haze and, perhaps, make the wine drinkable. On balance, it is probably best to discard such a wine. To avoid such a disaster in the future, eschew the use of copper in the winery.

For all metal hazes, the main cure is prevention. The use of glass, or plastic, during fermentation and maturation will obviate the problem. If the ingredient is very acid, then care is needed to minimise metal coming into contact with the must. So, if heat is indicated, use aluminium or, better still, stainless steel for all operations that involve heat. In this way, no metal will enter the wine and possibly spoil it.

Pectin Hazes

Pectin is a complex molecule made up of long chains of *galactonuric acid;* it has side chains of *methyl alcohol,* which are the source of the small amounts of methyl alcohol to be found in all wines. Pectin is an important part of the plant cell wall structure. When heated, it goes easily into solution, and 'gels' — a property used in the making of jams.

One advantage of using pectic enzyme preparations is that, because the enzyme breaks down the pectin, it follows that more of the fruit wall is destroyed. Thus, the yield of juice will be greater. But, beware. The chance of oxidation in the wine is increased unless strict anaerobic conditions are maintained.

If much more than a trace amount of pectin enters a wine, it will form a haze. Most fruit contain a small amount of *pectin destroying enzyme.* If this is not heated, it will help to prevent, or at least minimise, pectin hazes. (Do not forget that heating, as well as increasing the amount of pectin in solution, will destroy any protein).

Thus, the avoidance of heat during must preparation will reduce the chances of a haze. If, however, you use a fruit that has a high pectin content, it is probably wiser to use a commercial pectin destroying enzyme. If any 'additive' is taboo, then use no heat during must preparation.

If you suspect that there is a pectin haze in a wine, take 15 mls of *Methylated spirit* and add it to 5 mls of the wine. Depending on how much pectin is present, clots will develop in the solution. If only a small quantity, it may take up to two hours for the changes to occur.

If the haze is due to pectin, your only 'cure' is time. The haze will probably disappear — given a long enough maturation. Adding a gram or two of tannin may help the haze to clear because tannin is an acid with an opposite electrical charge to pectin.

Starch Hazes

Starch is a compound made up of thousands of glucose molecules joined together in chains. Because wine yeasts do not contain any enzyme capable of breaking down the starch, wines made from ingredients such as potatoes or grain will be likely to be hazy. Another likely wine to suffer from this is apple.

The use of a commercial preparation of *amylase,* the starch destroying enzyme, will avoid the problem. As with any protein, do not add it to a hot solution.

If you suspect a starch haze, take a small portion of wine and add one or two drops of *iodine.* If the solution turns any shade of purple, then the presence of starch is confirmed.

The treatment of this haze is with amylase. Again, do not add it to a hot solution. Carry out a test run on a small amount of the wine. This checks that the treatment works, and also allows you to see how much of the enzyme will be needed to treat the whole batch of wine.

Using tannin may increase the effectiveness of the enzyme; or it may prove a sufficient cure alone — thus avoiding 'additives'.

It is possible to minimise the likelihood of a starch haze by the use of *Diastatic Malt Extract* in your recipes if a starch haze seems likely. Using it in the *Starter Bottle* will provide a fair amount of the enzyme in the must; thus reducing the chances of a starch haze.

Finings

These are compounds that are used to remove a haze from a wine. Thus, we might call amylase and pektolase (pectic enzyme) types of finings. However, correctly speaking, finings are colloidal substances added to the wine (or beer) that will react with the haze causing compound to make it fall out of solution.

There are several *naturally occurring* substances widely used — such as *albumin* (or egg white), *gelatin, casein, bentonite,* and even blood. To these may be added sulphite (another reason for using this in winemaking), and tannin. The last is also a natural substance, but many prefer not to use any 'man made chemicals'.

Bentonite is a clay which carries a negative electrical charge. The bentonite combines with the haze causing compound to precipitate it out of solution. This clay has one advantage over all other fining agents; it is virtually impossible to over-fine when using it.

Perhaps the best for the 'natural' winemaker is a gelatin-tannin mixture. Make a 1% solution of the gelatin — taking care not to overheat the mixture. Add between 1 and 2 gms of tannin.

Before treating the bulk of the wine, carry out a trial fining to see how much of the mixture is required. Excess use will lead to discolouration, off-flavours, and *hazes.*

Albumin is an excellent fining agent. Its one drawback is that a minute amount will clear a large volume of wine; hence, over-fining is a common problem when using it.

All winemakers will have noticed that red wines clear far better and more quickly than white wines. This is due to their greater tannin content. So, it is easy to understand why tannin is often advocated as either the fining agent or an adjunct to it.

For the winemaker dedicated to non-use of 'additives', it is probably best to use gelatin or bentonite.

Finally, if none of the above ideas appeal, there remains only time as the cure. If winter is near, then the cold can be called in to help. Low temperature reduces the solubility of many substances and, therefore, can aid in wine clearing.

Brewers, too, have 'additives' to put in their beers. The various types of sugar may be considered 'pure'.

Water treatments used are based upon natural ingredients like calcium sulphate, magnesium sulphate, or even table salt, all of which are natural additives.

Irish Moss is used to help precipitate the protein in the barley and to ensure a clear beer. This is a seaweed which is not only natural product, but is also a herbal plant used in the treatment of chest and digestive complaints.

One of the most commonly used brewing finings is gelatine — again a natural product.

5 Sweetening your Wines and Beers

Despite the ban on free sugar for diabetics, it is still possible for them to enjoy a sweet wine. The limit imposed on the total permitted sugar is insufficient to make a wine adequate in alcohol content while containing enough residual sugar to sweeten it. Adhering to the limits set would lead to a very thin bodied wine with little, if any taste!

The most important point about making sweet wines is that the wine must be planned to be sweet. Do not think that sweetening up a dry wine will be a success. Because sweet wines need to be fuller flavoured, fuller bodied, and to have a greater acid content than dry wines, any attempt to 'doctor' a dry wine is doomed.

Do not, as is suggested in some books, heat the wine and then dissolve sugar or honey in it. The effect of heat is to caramelise (or burn) some of the sugar, a fault in a wine which is not pleasant — unless trying to make a *Madeira* type wine. Not only will this exceed the limits imposed on the sugar content, it will also produce a 'wine' which is distinctively inappropriately flavoured.

To reach the goal of fuller body and flavour, it is necessary to add more of the basic ingredients. In order to ensure that the wine is *balanced* (i.e. all the elements of taste are in harmony), the acid level of the must has to be increased. Table 3 gives suggested levels of acidity for different wine styles. This extra acid will counteract the sweetness of the finished wine.

In order to sweeten a diabetic wine, the use of free sugar has to be banned. Instead, artificial sweeteners must be used — the most commonly known one being *Saccharin* of which there are many commercial brands available — nearly all based on *Saccharin sodium.*

The simplest approach is to examine the different substances available to us in turn and then try to decide the best for our purposes.

Saccharin

Saccharin was the first artificial sweetening agent to be discovered. It is a benzoic acid derivative and is about 550 times as sweet as sugar. Pure saccharin is soluble in alcohol to the extent of about 3%; and is also soluble in *glycerine*. At room temperature, it is only slightly soluble in water.

It is widely used as a sweetening agent, particularly for diabetic diets where it is *the* substitute for sugar. It is also used in general dieting by those people with a sweet tooth who need to reduce both calories and their weight!

The use of saccharin in a dieter's drink means that the daily calorific intake can be reduced by a not inconsiderable amount. Its lack of food value helps weight loss.

The normal rate at which 'saccharin' is used to sweeten a drink is about 10 parts of saccharin to 1000 parts of the drink.

Saccharin, itself, has a very nasty after taste, especially when used to excess. It is about 550 times as sweet as glucose, but only when in a dilute solution. As the concentration becomes stronger, the taste becomes less obviously sweet until, in higher concentrations, it becomes positively bitter.

The sodium salt is not so bitter as the pure substance — hence its commercial use. It is also more soluble in water than the pure substance; but slightly less in alcohol. It is not as sweet as its parent — a mere 300 times as sweet as sugar!

Sorbitol

Like saccharin, sorbitol is a non fermentable sweetening agent. This means that it is not metabolised in the body, and, therefore, from the diabetic point of view, does not cause a rise in the blood sugar. Thus, it is safe for diabetics to use in their diets — up to a limit of about 30 gms per day. In this respect, sorbitol differs from other sweetening agents in that there is a limit to its use.

Sorbitol is very soluble in water, but only slightly in alcohol. As far as its 'sweetness' is concerned, it is only about as half as sweet as sugar.

Despite the fact that this 'sugar' is non-fermentable, diabetics need to excercise great care when using it. If they exceed the limit, the sorbitol may cause a rise in the blood sugar level with the consequent problems that this brings. This is particularly true if the disease is not under proper control.

Another 'ill-effect' of excess use of sorbitol is its action on the bowels. It has a marked laxative action. Diabetics, especially if their blood sugar level is raised, tend to a looseness of the bowels which will be aggravated by the use of sorbitol as a sweetening agent.

Mannitol

A compound which is an *isomer* of sorbitol. This means that it has the same chemical formula. It is also essentially the same shape of molecule — at least, in chemical terms! It has a bitter taste and can be the product of a *Malo-Lactic Fermentation*. Because of its taste, it is probably better not used as a sweetening agent.

Canderel

This is a commercial sweetener based upon plant protein. Again, it is not absorbed by the body, and so does not interfere with metabolism. Personally, I have not tried it for sweetening wines or beers, but it is certainly worth experimenting with. However, there is no data to suggest how long a wine sweetened with this will keep without developing off-flavours.

Lactose

The main sugar in milk. It is made up of glucose and another sugar called *galactose*. It is broken down by an enzyme called *lactase;* since yeasts do not secrete this enzyme, it is thus a non-fermentable sugar and of use as a sweetening agent — despite it being only one-third as sweet as sugar.

From its use in brewing as a sweetener for some stouts, comes the now illegal beer name of *Milk Stout.* However, from the winemaking point of view it is probably of limited value because of the amount required to adjust the sweetness. Many recipes for sweet stout do include it.

Glycerine

As one of the major by-products of fermentation, glycerine, plays an important role in the fermentation of sugar to alcohol. Not only does it play a large part in the smoothness of a wine, but it also has a sweet taste. While it is not possible to sweeten a wine with glycerine alone, its use in small amounts — perhaps 5-10 mls per gallon — particularly in an astringent wine, helps sweeten as well as conferring a roundness on it.

Sugar

When making 'normal' wines and beers, the usual method of sweetening is to include extra sugar in the recipe. Should you not wish to use the various substances already listed, and not be too bothered about the calorific content, the usual method of making sweet wines can be employed.

Unlike the method for 'healthy wines' where the wine is sweetened after fermentation to dryness, a sweet wine with residual sugar has to have the sugar added either in stages throughout fermentation or all at the outset. It is better to add the sugar in stages to minimise the chances of the fermentation sticking. Sweet wines made this way will have a higher alcohol content, as well as more body. Which method you choose is an entirely personal choice.

Making a Sweetening Solution

If you decide to ferment to dryness and then add sweeteners, the choice lies between saccharin and the new protein based agent. I have never used it myself, but it is well worth experimenting with — particularly if it proves less bitter in higher concentrations.

My own choice is one of the saccharin sodium preparations — *Sweetex*. There are, of course, many other brands available. The main consideration is that it should be a liquid. Tablets and powder are not recommended for wine or beer making. They contain preservative compounds which can cause colour changes or hazes in the finished product. These compounds are entirely harmless but will detract from the appearance of the wine or beer!

The liquids are concentrated saccharin sodium in a solution of *propylene glycol,* (E450), as a preservative. This is prepared from seaweed, and is a natural product. It is not absorbed into the body and has no known ill-effects. It is also safe for diabetics to use.

Sweetex liquid is available in bottles of 28.4 mls — to the non-metric this is one fluid ounce! Each bottle has the sweetening equivalent of about $2\frac{1}{2}$ lbs of sugar. In other words, one bottle is the same as a one gallon sugar solution with a SG of 90. This compares with the gravity of 300 for the 'normal' sugar solution used by winemakers made from 1 lb of sugar in 1 pint of water. (1 kg/1 litre).

For the diabetic, the advantage of using a substance like Sweetex is that it contains only 118 calories per bottle — compared with almost 4500 calories in an equivalent weight of sugar.

The strength of the liquid artificial sweeteners is such that excessive use is extremely hazardous — overuse can easily ruin a wine.

Take heed from this cautionary tale. When sweetening a brown ale, I successfully ruined it by adding 6 *drops* to a 2 gallon batch. It resulted in a hideously oversweet beer with a dreadful, bitter after taste.

To avoid such a *fiasco,* make a dilution. Obtain a 5 or 10 ml dropper bottle from your local chemist. Clean and sterilise thoroughly before a final rinsing with sulphite solution. Do not use boiling water or sulphite on the rubber of the dropper since this can cause perishing.

Place 5 or 10 drops of saccharin solution in the bottle — i.e. 1 drop per 1 ml. Add 2 drops of glycerine as a preservative because the propylene already present is going to be diluted. Now add the appropriate number of mls of water sulphited at the rate of 100 ppm.

This sweetening solution has a shelf life of several months without any obvious deterioration, in my experience. Provided distilled or purified water is used there will be no deposit formation.

Sweetening Wines and Beers

Take a portion of wine, or beer, say 100 mls. To this, add the sweetening solution one drop at a time. Between each addition, taste the result. Always keep a reference sample of the wine or beer, so that, in case of doubt, you can check to see just exactly how the original tasted.

If in doubt as to the effect of an addition, wait; and return to it at a later time to retaste it.

Do not forget that after a surprisingly short time, the palate becomes jaded and cannot accurately tell small differences in the taste of wines and beers. So, do not rush the job, take your time to ensure that the end result is to your liking.

Keep a careful note of how many drops you have added because there is nothing so infuriating (or sloppy, in an experimental sense), than to arrive at the perfect answer only to discover that you have no idea of its composition.

Once the wine or beer is sweetened to your satisfaction, it is easy to work out how many drops of the sweetening solution are required to sweeten the bulk.

The long term effect of artificial sweetening agents on wines and beers is not known, so it is not possible to say just exactly how long they can be kept. As we have seen, the wines we are making are lower in alcohol than their commercial counterparts, and so they will have a shorter life. Err on the side of caution. Do not keep these wines more than a year without checking that they are still drinkable before serving. Experience will show exactly how long your wines will keep; but it is my belief that they will develop off-flavours if kept for too long because saccharin is slowly oxidised over a period of time.

Beers do not have this problem of keeping, since they are nearly always drunk within a short time of maturing.

There is, however, no need for such a statement to raise alarm since saccharin is a 'safe substance'. It is related to *benzoic acid*, and should, in theory, help inhibit secondary fermentation in both wines and beers.

Do not forget that the addition of sulphite is important, both as an anti-oxidant and a preservative, as well as an antiseptic against infection and refermentation. If you wish to use it, do so at the normal rates to your wines, but beware of excess use. Some diabetic drugs can combine with sulphite and thus interfere with the control of the condition.

6 To Add or not to Add? – That is the Question

A few years ago a friend came into my winery and complained bitterly about 'all the chemicals' there were on the shelf. At first sight he had more than a point; there were, and are, a vast number of jars and bottles! However, on going through each in turn, I was able to persuade him that most, if not all, are natural substances. Many are prepared from nature, the rest pure substances, laboratory prepared it is true, but free from any other 'additives'.

Additives, in a winemaking sense, are different from some substances added to our food. Most are naturally occurring substances prepared to a high degree of purity. Hence, they convey no danger to the ingester, and all are a part of our diet.

While I am quite happy to continue wine and beer making in the same way, I am well aware that many people have an increasing dislike of adding any substance, beyond the basic ingredients, to anything of their own making. Respecting this desire I intend to try to give recipes that cater for both viewpoints, using natural ingredients where ever possible. For those who prefer the 'modern' way I shall also list the essential additives, or alternative methods of achieving the same results.

To go back to the beginning, just what is an additive?

For our purposes, an additive can be defined as any substance that is added to a wine or a beer other than the basic ingredients. Their purpose is to prevent the fermentation 'sticking' (or stopping prematurely), an important consideration when we are making sugar free wines and beers; or natural enzymes to prevent haze formation.

In essence they are foodstuffs for yeast growth (apart from sugar) or yeast enzyme activity which will ensure a healthy fermentation with the minimum amount of fusel oil production.

Ammonium salts – either the phosphate or sulphate – are

used to provide nitrogen to help the yeast grow. Absence of nitrogen means that the yeast will, in effect, turn cannibal and destroy dead yeast cells to provide at least some of the needed nitrogen. Unfortunately, this *autolysis,* as it is called, leads to the formation of fusel oils. These are higher alcohols which give the wine a foul taste, and also cause hangovers.

Magnesium is needed by the yeast for some of the chemical reactions that occur during fermentation. If you have hard water, there is probably enough in the water for a healthy fermentation. However, for certain beers, and in soft water areas, magnesium should be added. The most convenient form available is *Epsom Salts,* widely used as a bowel medicine by many people.

Next, we have to consider *Vitamin B_1.* This is essential for fermentation, and especially yeast reproduction. Vitamins are a part of the diet that we all need because we are, on the whole, unable to make these substances in our bodies ourselves. Similarly with yeasts.

In addition to these 'foodstuffs' we have to consider other 'un-natural' ingredients.

The most important is the *Acid* required; firstly for fermentation, and secondly for taste.

If one wishes there are available the basic wine acids: *Tartaric, Malic,* and *Citric.* They are reasonably cheap, and have the advantage that you can measure precise amounts to adjust your wine to the correct level of acidity for fermentation and the finished wine. The alternative to using these acids is to use either *Lemon Juice* or a fruit with a high natural acidity.

Other substances used include additives to prevent hazes in the finished wine. *Pectic Enzyme,* to remove pectin, and *Amylase,* the starch destroying enzyme. While most wines will clear given time (often a very long time!), most winemakers are impatient to sample their wares and will not wait for them to clear naturally.

If you are adamant about using only ingredients from nature, is there a way in which these additives can be left out of the recipes?

Very few vegetables or fruit contain large amounts of nitrogen. The obvious exception is grain. However, grain is a difficult ingredient to use for winemaking, and leaves us with the problem of starch hazes; the only cure for which is, as previously noted, time, or another additive — *Amylase.*

Apricots, Blackberries, Dried Currants, Grapes, Greengages, Dried Peaches, Prunes, and Rhubarb are the only fruit with any appreciable amount of protein in them. Carrots, Peas, Potatoes, and Spinach, the only vegetables. Of course, this is with reference to winemaking ingredients.

The amount of ammonium salts that one usually adds to a wine is of the order of $\frac{1}{6}$ oz per gallon, (5 gms per 5 litres). Each of the vegetables and fruit listed above contains at least 7 gms per 100 gms of ingredient. In other words if used in normal winemaking amounts, they would provide enough material for the yeast to grow healthily, and can be considered good ingredients to ensure sufficient nitrogen for the yeast to make the protein it requires.

Magnesium is found most abundantly in Dried Apricots, Dried Figs, and Spinach. The trouble is that the amount of each ingredient required to yield enough magnesium recommended for healthy fermentation is more than a wine requires. However, grapes manage entirely satisfactory fermentation and they contain about one-tenth of the magnesium of the fruit and vegetables I have listed. So, we can, therefore, probably leave magnesium out of our list of additives — especially if the water supply is hard since that will contain a fair amount of this 'additive'.

Some of the biochemical compounds which we need we cannot synthesise ourselves; but they are needed for various functions of our bodies. Such substances are called *Vitamins*.

Vitamins are compounds essential for healthy life. All living matter needs them in varying amounts. Much of our body is created by taking in food which is then broken down to its component 'parts'. These are then reformed into the different compounds which make up the human body.

Yeasts are no different from us — they too need vitamins. The most important for fermentation is vitamin B_1. It is required as a catalyst (or speeding agent for a chemical reaction) during the conversion of sugar to alcohol. It is, therefore, a necessary additive to achieve ideal conditions for fermentation. As the tablets are made in metric sizes, the recommended amount is one or two 3 mg tablets per gallon (or 5 litres) depending on the basic wine ingredients. As a pure medicine we have no worries about other 'additives' being present in the tablet.

Finally, we come to the haze preventing compounds. These are *Amylase*, the enzyme which breaks down starch; and *Pectic Enzyme*, which breaks down pectin.

Starch hazes may cause a problem in wines made from cereals, potatoes, and apples, unless precautions are taken to prevent this trouble. Since beers do not suffer from this defect, we can take a lesson from this, and use *Diastatic Malt Extract* in the must. Not only will this provide nutrients for the yeast, but the enzymes present will break down the starch; thus preventing haze formation.

Pectin is a substance found in all fruit in greater or lesser amounts where it is an important component in cell wall structure. It is soluble in hot water. Hence the use of heat to extract flavour, colour, and juice, will increase the pectin content of a wine. Most fruit have a small amount of pectin destroying enzyme on their surface which, provided no heat is used (which destroys protein), will help minimise pectin haze formation.

Most wine recipes advocate the use of one of the commercially available *Pectin Destroying Enzyme* preparations. However, if we are trying to avoid the use of 'additives' we have to ensure that the minimum quantity of pectin gets into the must.

To this end, use no method involving heat for ingredient extraction. Careful selection of ingredients will also help reduce the problem. Grapes, when ripe, contain a large amount of pectic enzymes. Despite this, pectic enzyme is used routinely in many commercial winemaking enterprises in order to ensure clear wines. Apparently, this is also of benefit to the smoothness of the finished wine.

So, to summarise. If you wish to use additives the following are recommended at the accompanying rates.

TABLE 5

List of Additives for Wines

Additive	Amount/gallon	Amount/5 litres
Ammonium phosphate	$\frac{1}{2}$ oz	15 gms
Potassium phosphate	$\frac{1}{4}$ oz	7.5 gms
Magnesium sulphite	$\frac{1}{30}$ oz	1 gm

If, however, you wish to avoid the use of additives, use.

Malt Extract or Marmite	$\frac{1}{6}$ oz	5 gms

Please note that the additives for wines are not given with each recipe. Instead, use the lists given above. Each recipe does, however, refer you to this page.

Sulphite is the general term used by winemakers and brewers for *metabisulphite*. It is their main sterlising agent. Its ill effects are discussed in Chapter 13.

Most winemakers use it at one or more stages of making a wine. Either for sterilising the must; or ensuring sterility and aiding maturing at the end of fermentation. As it is so common, the final choice must lie with yourself as to whether to use or not.

What is most important is that, if you choose not to use sulphite, you take great care to ensure sterility at all stages of winemaking and brewing.

7 Gladden Thine Heart!

Heart disease is now one of the greatest medical problems facing the civilised world and accounts for over one-third of deaths in this country. How can these deaths be reduced?

Like so many problems in life, the best method of cure is prevention. If one can keep one's blood pressure down and, by eating sensibly, prevent 'furring' of the arteries, the solution can be almost complete.

Throughout life, the arteries, having started out as elastic tubes, become thicker and stiffer. If excess food is eaten, one of the most dangerous places it is stored, (after this food is changed into fat by the body) is in the walls of the arteries.

Because the *Cholesterol,* (the form in which this fat is stored), is not laid down in a regular pattern, but rather in lumps here and there, it follows that the normal flow of blood is interrupted. Concomitant with this, and perhaps more importantly, the usually smooth lining of the arteries is destroyed. This *Atheroma,* as it is called, can lead to blood clots forming on these lumps of cholesterol. This in turn may lead to the occlusion of a blood vessel, or a clot may break free and cause a stroke.

The outcome of this is dependant upon the site of the blockage. In the leg it may be gangrene. In the heart, a heart attack; if one of the main heart arteries is affected, it may cause death.

If a clot forms on the inside of a blood vessel it may break off and travel around the body causing equally serious problems, the most disastrous, perhaps, being a stroke.

It used to be said that heavy drinking caused *Arterio-sclerosis* as this narrowing and hardening of the arteries is called. However, examining the blood vessels of such people, shows that they are actually less affected than non-drinkers. Also, as alcohol dissolves fat, it follows that alcohol can help stop this process by breaking down some of the cholesterol.

In recent years *cholesterol* has become one of the 'in words'.

As a result of various researchers showing its dangers, eggs, cheese, milk, many meats, and desserts are banned in some households. (Almost as limiting a diet as some very strict vegetarians.)

However, rational thought and sensible eating will reduce the risks of arterio-sclerosis attendant upon high cholesterol in the blood. Luckily, many of the 'bad foods' are luxuries so that they are only infrequently eaten. Probably the best way of keeping the level down *(unless specifically ordered otherwise)* is by the use of *polyunsaturated fats;* i.e. sunflower oil for cooking, or the many brands of genuinely unsaturated fat spreads. But, beware! Many of the vegetable oils, for example *rape oil,* in fact contain highly saturated fats.

As the arteries harden, the blood pressure rises. To this must be added the increase, all too often seen with increasing years and seniority, in 'tension'. (Later we will see the part that alcohol can play in reducing tension). However the *moderate* drinking of a lightly sulphited (or not if you prefer to keep 'additives' out of your wines) wine can lower the blood pressure appreciably by its action on the brain.

Often, before a heart attack, a patient may suffer from *Angina* – a tight pain in the chest. This is a warning that all is not well with the heart. Although this pain may preceed a heart attack, it does not inevitably lead to this. The warning should be taken seriously, and you should see your doctor.

Until the discovery of such modern drugs like *G.T.N.,* (or *Glyceryl Trinitrate* in full), alcohol was used to treat this condition. Even today, *in an emergency (and only if other drugs are not available),* it can be life saving by increasing the action of the heart, lowering high blood pressure, relieving pain, and reducing tension.

This is one of the few occasions in which spirits are, medicinally speaking, better than wines or beers. The higher alcohol content means that some alcohol is absorbed through the lungs in the form of vapour so that the drug can act more quickly than if merely swallowed.

To show the benefit of alcohol in the prevention of heart disease, an American specialist carried out a survey. The results showed that, although alcohol neither caused nor prevented angina, excess drinking was rare in sufferers. In some patients alcohol was shown to be the most helpful drug in relieving the attacks of pain.

It is, however, most important to realise that continued drinking during an attack could prove fatal because alcohol, after first relieving the pain and then relaxing the patient, can go on to cause depression of the action of the nerves to the heart and breathing centres in the brain.

If angina (or chest pain) is succeeded by a heart attack, the use of moderate amounts of alcohol can be beneficial. Although one scientist has shown that there is no action of alcohol on the heart to account for this relief, alcohol probably reduces the amount of work the heart has to do by lowering the blood pressure. Again, he drew attention to the relaxing effect of alcohol.

Some vascular conditions causing spasm of the blood vessels (diseases like *Raynaud's phenomenon and Buerger's disease* — both of which cause pain in the fingers and toes in particular) can also be helped by the *vasodilating* effect of alcohol.

There is, in fact, very little scientific evidence to support these hypotheses; and indeed, in many textbooks, the use of alcohol in heart disease is taboo. However, logically speaking, and in the light of statistical evidence, it seems likely that moderate use (the keyword throughout the book!) of alcohol may very well reduce the incidence of heart disease.

Even if, scientifically speaking, alcohol is valueless, enjoy a drink in the knowledge that, apart from the pleasure, it could be prolonging your life!

We now need to consider just which wines or beers can be considered 'the best' in cases of heart disease. Firstly it seems that the prime consideration is a well-aged wine because the esters and aldehydes that develop during aging play a large part in the actions of 'alcohol' on the circulation. Alcohol by itself does not play a consistent rôle in the heart's physiology. It can, just to be awkward, either increase or decrease the blood flow!

Even in ancient China, the use of wines with *Angelica, Zingiber* (ginger), and *Cinnamon* dissolved in them was the recommended treatment for heart problems. A French physician concocted a mixture of juniper berries, squill and digitalis to 'cure symptoms of heart disease'; digitalis being incontrovertibly a cardiac drug.

The situation is different when we come to look at the Juniper family. *Juniperus communis* (the common juniper) is carminative in action (i.e. it soothes the action of the intestines).

However, as it causes contraction of the smooth muscle fibres of the heart, it would seem to be contraindicated in heart or vascular disease, despite its diuretic action − the removal of excess fluid from the body.

Juniperus macropoda was also used in some pharmacopoeiae. Cedar Wood Oil, obtained from *J. virginiana,* is used in perfumery − hardly a medicinal use! Other species of the juniper are used for ointments or creams for the treatment of skin conditions like *Psoriasis.*

One species *J. sabina,* is said to have great effect in the treatment of asthma. Again, there is little evidence to support this family in the treatment of heart disease. So, presumably, gin can be ruled out as the spirit of choice. Indeed, brandy has been shown to be the best in the treatment of acute attacks of vascular disease. From this, it seems logical to exclude the juniper berry from 'heart wines'.

Cardamons, another carminative drug, was used to flavour purgatives. In addition it is soothing to the muscles of the intestine and so can help prevent colicky pains.

Angelica is of value in chest conditions. Again, no cardiac action unless one considers a condition called *Cardiac Asthma* where it may be of value in helping the patient get rid of phlegm.

Commercial wines claimed to aid prevention of heart attacks are *Champagne* because of the *potassium tartrate* present. However, since this salt precipitates out of solution at a fairly low concentration, this is unlikely to play any great part in the prevention or cure of disease. Presumably, the theory behind the claim is that potassium is vital for the proper working of the nerves and the heart.

Claims that *Muscadet* is of value in preventing arteriosclerosis must be viewed with suspicion. The suggestion is that, since the soil whereon the grapes are grown is low in calcium, so too is the wine. In practice, wines cannot contain large amounts of calcium tartrate because it precipitates out of solution above a low concentration.

Books dealing with herbalism list the following plants as having properties useful for the treatment of heart or circulatory conditions. Some of these plants have constituents used in formal medicine. Others have no obvious value − speaking pharmacologically. The first thing to establish, before going any farther, is which of them is safe to use in winemaking.

It cannot be stressed strongly enough that many herbs listed in this book are toxic — and hence, dangerous to use. If in doubt about whether any plant, or part of it, is poisonous — **DO NOT USE IT.**

First let us see which plants listed are safe:

'SAFE' HERBS THAT MAY ACT ON THE HEART

Arnica	Catmint	Juniper
Ash	Chamomile	Limeflower
Asparagus	Coltsfoot	Meadowsweet
Birch	Dandelion	Nettle
Blackcurrant	Fennel	Parsley Piert
Broom	Ginger	Raspberry
Burdock	Hawthorn	Woodruff
	Hops	Yarrow

Any other plant should be considered dangerous and should never be used by the amateur winemaker, either for winemaking or to make extracts to cure his or her own ills.

There are several words that are probably unfamiliar to many non herbalists that we shall meet in this chapter. It is worth defining them.

Cardioactive is the word used to describe a plant or its active ingredient that has an action on the heart.

Circulatory Stimulant is commonly used of plants which act on the blood vessels and increase the flow of blood through them.

A *Diuretic* is any plant (or drug) that aids the heart by removing excess fluid from the body. These may be used in heart failure, or chest conditions. Their use (as suggested in some herbal books) in conditions like kidney stones or infections must be considered suspect.

Many herbal diuretics are based on a group of chemicals known as *Flavinoids*. These same chemicals are also said to heal the lining of the blood vessels.

Vasodilators are drugs or plants that cause the blood vessels to dilate.

While some of these herbs have a useful temperature

lowering effect, their main use is in dilating blood vessels suffering from various diseases that cause a poor circulation.

To return to the list of 'safe' herbs. A selection of recipes for wines using them follows. Because the listed herbs may be of use in other systems, a reference will be given to find the recipe if it does not appear here. Some of the herbs listed have dubious winemaking uses — they are omitted.

Herbal Uses and Recipes

Asparagus

The tips are recommended by Culpeper infused in wine for sciatica. The root was used to aid the eyesight. The fresh juice is considered useful as a diuretic (a drug which rids the body of excess water; and in the treatment of gout. A simple recipe for this wine is as follows.

★ Asparagus Wine

Ingredient	Quantity per gallon	Quantity per 5 litres
Asparagus	4 lbs	2 kgs
Lemon	1 medium size	1 medium size
Orange	1 medium size	1 medium size
Barley	1 lb	500 gms
Sugar	to SG 70	to SG 70
Vitamin B_1	6 mg	6 mg
Yeast		
Water	to volume	to volume

For the recommended additives, see Page 53.

Boil the asparagus, lemon and orange, chopped or diced, in 2 pints (1 litre) of water with the barley for about 10 minutes. Strain through a muslin bag into the fermentation vat. Take the SG when the mixture has cooled — do not forget the temperature correction — and add the permitted amount of sugar.

Add the nutrients and when cool pitch an active yeast starter. When fermentation has died down, make to volume and ferment to dryness under air lock.

Rack, and mature. Sweeten to taste as described in Chapter 5.

Birch Sap

An ointment or cream made from the oil extracted from the Birch is still in the Pharmacopoeia; and there is still a commercial medical preparation available.

The linament used by sportsmen and women *Oil of Wintergreen* is almost identical to the oil obtained from the birch.

Many parts of the Silver Birch tree are used in herbal treatments. From the winemaker's point of view, the only part of the tree that we can use is the sap, from which can be made one of the most popular wines early in the year.

To harvest the sap, use a 1″ (2.5 cm) bit to drill a hole *just beyond the bark;* not deep into the tree (this may kill it). Place a bored cork with a suitable plastic tube in it into the hole. Lead the tube into a collecting jar whose neck has been plugged with cotton wool.

After approximately 48 hours, you will have collected up to six pints (3.75 litres) of sap. After this time drive a *hard wood* plug into your hole. This means that, most importantly, the tree will not die; and, secondly, you can use the tree year after year; harvesting it for your wines.

✶ Birch Sap Wine

Ingredient	Quantity per gallon	Quantity per 5 litres
Birch Sap	6 pints	3.75 litres
Grapefruit concentrate	5 oz	140 mls
Sugar	to SG 70	to SG 70
Citric acid	$\frac{1}{2}$ oz	15 gms
Grape tannin	$\frac{1}{2}$ teaspoon	2.5 gms
Vitamin B_1	6 mg	6 mg
Champagne Yeast		
Water	to volume	to volume

For the recommended additives, see Page 53.

Mix all the ingredients except sugar and check the SG. If within limits, add the permitted sugar. Add an active yeast starter. When fermentation has died down, make to volume; and ferment to dryness under air lock.

Rack and mature for six months at least. This wine can improve over as long as two years. Sweeten to taste when bottling or before drinking.

Blackcurrant

Recommended by herbalists as an aid to reducing temperatures and for reducing oedema. Lozenges made from the juice are excellent for soothing coughs and colds, as is Blackcurrant 'tea' made from blackcurrant jelly. The syrup still has a place in *Martindale* for its use in the symptomatic treatment of coughs and sore throats; otherwise, its main use is in syrups as a source of *Vitamin C.*

⋆ Blackcurrant Wine

Ingredient	Quantity per gallon	Quantity per 5 litres
Blackcurrants	3 lbs	1.3 kgs
Sugar	To SG 70	to SG70
Citric acid	1 teaspoon	5 gms
Vitamin B_1	6 mg	6 mg
Water	to volume	to volume

For the recommended additives, see Page 53.

Place the blackcurrants into a large pan, crush them, and add 4 pints (2 litres) or water. Measure the specific gravity, and dissolve the permitted amount of sugar in the rest of the water. When cool, add the nutrients, and add an active yeast starter. When fermentation has died down, make to volume.

Ferment to dryness under air lock. Rack and mature for at least three months before racking again into bottle — sweetening if required as described in Chapter 5.

Broom

As well as treating excess fluid in heart failure, broom is of value in the treatment of irregular heart rhythms. An infusion made from the dried shoot tips was in the *British Pharmacopoeia* in 1898. Before then, an alcoholic infuson was made from the plant tips and used to treat oedema; and is still listed in the pharmacopoeia.

✳ Broom Wine

Ingredient	Quantity per gallon	Quantity per 5 litres
Broom flowers	2 pints	1 litre
Sugar	to SG 70	to SG 70
Acid	to 4.5 ppt	to 4.5 ppt
Vitamin B_1	6 mg	6 mg
Water	to volume	to volume

For the recommended additives, see Page 53.

Pick the flowers on a sunny day. Use them as fresh as possible — before they lose their scent. Remove all the calyces, ('green bits'), in order to prevent a bitter taste in the finished wine. Wash the flowers by rinsing in a colander and then place them in 6 pints (3 litres) of water. In order to ensure that the flowers are sterile, add two Campden tablets to the water. Add the permitted sugar — flower petals have no sugar, so that there is no need to test the SG, nutrients, and acid. If you prefer, use the juice of one lemon instead of the acid crystals. Press the flowers below the surface of the water and leave for twenty four hours.

The next day, add the sugar which you have dissolved in the remainder of the water. This done at the same time as the flowers are prepared means that the temperature of the must will be correct for the adding of the yeast.

Ferment for one week before straining the flowers off. Ferment to dryness under air lock, having made up to volume once fermentation has died down. Rack and mature. Sweeten to taste as described in Chapter 5.

Burdock

The roots are used, as are the leaves and seeds. Apart from some action as a diuretic in the treatment of kidney conditions, the plant is also used for a cough remedy, and to settle indigestion. It is also considered to be a good 'cleanser' of the blood, although the pharmacopoeia now considers the plant to be of doubtful value.

⋆ Burdock Wine

Ingredient	Quantity per gallon	Quantity per 5 litres
Burdock leaves	1 lb	500 gms
Wine grape concentrate	1 pint	500 mls
Sugar	to SG 70	to SG 70
Vitamin B_1	6 mg	6 mg
Water	to volume	to volume

For the recommended additives, see Page 53.

Place all the ingredients in a bucket, add an active yeast starter, and ferment for one week before straining off the leaves. Once fermentation has died down, make to volume.

Ferment to dryness under air lock, rack and mature for several months. Before bottling, sweeten to taste as described in Chapter 5. This wine is probably best as a medium or sweet wine.

Dandelion

In addition to its action as a diuretic, the dandelion is used in the treatment of digestive, kidney and liver complaints. The roots are the part most often used in herbal treatments. From the roots, tinctures, extracts, and juices are prepared. The use of the plant was listed in all official pharmacopoeia until the turn of the century. Its main use is given here as being for fluid retention due to liver disease. It is still recognised as a *Bitter,* or digestive stimulant, in some cases of indigestion; and is also a mild laxative.

*   **Dandelion Wine**

Ingredient	Quantity per gallon	Quantity per 5 litres
Dandelion flowers	4 pints	2 litres
White grape concentrate	$\frac{1}{2}$ pint	250 mls
Sugar	to SG 70	to SG 70
Citric acid	1 teaspoon	7 gms
Vitamin B_1	6 mg	6 mg
Water	to volume	to volume

For the recommended additives, see Page 53.

Pick the flowers on a sunny day. Remove any green from below the florets. Place in a bucket with the other ingredients and nutrients. Mix thoroughly, and sulphite with one or two Campden tablets. Leave for twenty four hours before adding an active yeast starter.

After four days fermentation, strain off the flowers, make to volume, and continue fermentation under air lock to dryness. Rack and mature for up to as long as two years. Sweeten to taste as described in Chapter 5.

Ginger

Used in herbal treatments as a stimulant to the circulation, it is a dilator of the blood vessels. It was formerly used in general medicine as well for its action in soothing the gut. It is sometimes used in laxatives on the assumption that it prevents colic. Chiefly, it is used as a flavouring agent. Both these uses being given in the pharmacopoeia.

*   # Ginger Wine

Ingredient	Quantity per gallon	Quantity per 5 litres
Root ginger	3 oz	75 gms
White grape concentrate	½ pint	250 mls
Sugar	to SG 70	to SG 70
Bananas — skinned	2 lbs	1 kgm
Vitamin B$_1$	6 mg	6 mg
Water	to volume	to volume

For the recommended additives, see Page 53.

Chop the ginger roots into small pieces and place in a bucket with 5 pints (2.5 litres) of water. Place the skinned, chopped, bananas in a pan with 1 pint (500 mls) water. Boil until they are soft; strain the liquid into the bucket and add the other ingredients and nutrients. When cool, add an active yeast starter. After about ten days rack into a demi john, make to volume, and ferment to dryness under air lock. Rack again and mature for one year. Sweeten to taste as described in Chapter 5.

Hawthorn

Also known as *Mayflower,* this plant has a strong action on the heart. It dilates the blood vessels, and also slows down the rate of the heart beat. It used to be in the pharmacopoeia where it was recommended as a heart drug. It has now been removed as being of doubtful value.

*   # Mayflower Wine

Ingredient	Quantity per gallon	Quantity per 5 litres
Hawthorn Blossom	2 quarts	2 litres

Other ingredients and method as for *Dandelion* wine — page 65.

Limeflower

Used as a herbal treatment for high blood pressure, the flowers are also used as a treatment for tension. Herbally, either an infusion or a distillate is made from the flowers. Lime flowers are listed in the pharmacopoeia as being of use in the relief of colic and reducing temperatures.

✳ Limeflower Wine

Ingredient	Quantity per gallon	Quantity per 5 litres
Limeflowers	2 pints	1 litre

Other ingredients and method as for *Dandelion* wine. See page 65.

Meadowsweet

In addition to removing excess fluid from the body, Meadowsweet soothes the stomach. It can also be used to reduce temperatures, and as an anti-inflamatory agent; for this purpose the method of choice is an infuson of the herb in wine. This plant has never been included in official pharmacopoeia.

✳ Meadowsweet Wine

Ingredient	Quantity per gallon	Quantity per 5 litres
Meadowsweet flowers	1 gallon	4.5 litres
Raisins	1 lb	450 gms
Sugar	to SG 70	to SG 70
Tannin	$\frac{1}{30}$ oz	1 gm
Citric acid	$\frac{1}{2}$ oz	15 gms
Yeast		
Vitamin B$_1$	6 mg	6 mg
Water	to volume	to volume

For the recommended additives, see Page 53.

Pick the flowers on a dry sunny day. Only use the heads. Pour boiling water over the flowers. Chop the raisins and add them to the bucket. Add the permitted sugar; stir well to dissolve. When cool add the nutrients.

If you prefer, use the juice of three lemons instead of the citric acid; and a half pint (250 mls) of strong tea instead of the tannin.

Ferment on the pulp for one week. Stir the must each day to break up the cap that develops on the surface. Then rack, make to volume, and ferment to dryness under airlock. Rack and mature. Sweeten to taste as described in Chapter 5.

Nettle

Used herbally as a stimulant for the circulation, diuretic, and in diabetes to lower the blood sugar. It is also used in the herbal treatment of asthma. The plant has never appeared in the pharmacopoeia.

★ Nettle Wine

Ingredient	Quantity per gallon	Quantity per 5 litres
Young nettle tops	2 quarts	2.25 litres
White grape concentrate	$\frac{1}{2}$ pint	300 mls
Sugar	to SG 70	to SG 70
Citric acid	$\frac{1}{3}$ oz or 1 lemon	10 gms or 1 lemon
Sauternes yeast		
Vitamin B$_1$	6 mg	6 mg
Water	to volume	to volume

For the recommended additives, see Page 53.

Pour 4 pints (2 litres) of boiling water over the leaves. Cover and leave for twenty four hours. Strain off the liquid into a demi john. Add the grape concentrate, permitted sugar and additives. Add a further pint (500 mls) cold water and an active yeast starter.

When the fermentation dies down, make up to volume and ferment to dryness. Mature for up to two years. Sweeten to taste as described in Chapter 5. If you wish, add about an ounce (30 mls) glycerine. This will not only make the wine smoother, but will also emulate a *Sauternes*-type wine.

Yarrow

Used herbally to dilate the peripheral blood vessels, it has uses in reducing temperature. It is also used as an appetite stimulant, and to reduce colic. Another action is said to stop bleeding. It is listed in the pharmacopoeia as having all these properties.

✳ Yarrow Wine

Ingredient	Quantity per gallon	Quantity per 5 litres
Yarrow leaves and flowers	1 gallon	4.5 litres

Other ingredients and method as for *Nettle* Wine. See Page 68.

8 Wise Man or Fool?

What did Alexander the Great, Martin Luther, Sir Isaac Newton, John Milton, Dr Harvey, Dr Johnson, and King Louis XIV, all have in common? They all suffered from gout.

Sydenham, a physician in the seventeenth century was the first to describe the disease in modern times. *'It seems that more wise men than fools are victims',* he wrote.

Everyone who has seen cartoons will recognise instantly the typical picture of the eighteenth century squire. Dressed in his hunting pink, he is sitting in his winged arm chair. With a glass of port in his right hand, and decanter in the other, he repeatedly fills and empties the glass. His foot, encased in vast quantities of cotton wool, rests upon a footstool. The hour is improved to the beholder by the expression of anguish as a clumsy footman stumbles against the excruciatingly painful, gout afflicted foot.

The accurate part of these cartoons is the age of the sufferer and the site of his affliction. The agony is real; but the rest is not entirely true.

Gout may be amusing to the beholder; to the sufferer it is no joke. It is an extremely painful disease which affects the joints. Most commonly, the joint of the big toe; although it can occur in any joint of the hand or foot. It is not uncommon to see it in the elbow. And it can also affect the earlobe.

In fact this disease affects parts of the body that undergo repeated trauma. The commonest sufferer is indeed the middle-aged man — as portrayed in our cartoon — but no-one is exempt.

Gout is caused by the deposition of *Uric Acid crystals* in affected joints. It is a disease that has been well chronicled throughout history and was even described by the physicians of ancient Rome and Greece. Although it can be hereditary, it is usually not. However, it is inarguably associated with many of the diseases of so-called civilisation, such as high blood pressure and arterial disease.

Environment and genetics do play a part in the origin of the disease. A study carried out amongst the Maoris of New Zealand and a remote Pacific island called Puka Puka showed that gout is twice as common in the men of New Zealand as in the menfolk of that island so far from 'civilisation'.

Gout is rare in women, and Hippocrates noted that it was unknown in eunuchs.

To return to our cartoon, it was noticed in the eighteenth century that indulgence in the large meals characteristic of those days, associated with the great amounts of alcohol drunk, was often an overture to an attack of the disease. As a result of this, dietary restrictions were imposed on gout sufferers. When uric acid was eventually proved to be the causative agent, this appeared to give credence to the dietary treatment of the condition.

The rationale was that the metabolism of food by the body caused the production of uric acid. As the body could not get rid of any excess of the acid, it was deposited in the joints causing an attack.

It has now been shown that most of the uric acid present in the body is formed by the body itself, and is not dependant upon diet alone to produce it. Thus, once a tablet had been discovered which could treat the condition, diet itself became of secondary importance.

It is indisputable that gout is a disease of the wealthy due, no doubt in part, to their extra rich diet and greater alcohol intake. To support this hypothesis, it was noticed that in Germany, after the Second World War, the disease was virtually unknown. Obesity is certainly a predisposing factor — a pointer to ally the condition to the theory of a dietary origin.

More recently it has been noticed that there was an increase in incidence of the disease among the Professorial staff and managerial classes in the City of Edinburgh. This prompted the hypothesis that a moderately raised level of uric acid may be a stimulant to the brain. *Caffeine,* the stimulant in coffee and tea, only differs slightly from uric acid in structure.

Looking again at the cartoon, we see that it is always port or madeira that is depicted as the guilty party in causing gout. Thus, it is always these drinks which get 'the blame'.

This is probably due to the fact that the upper classes of the eighteenth century (as we have seen, nearly always the afflicted class) almost always drank one or both of these beverages. In those days an Englishman never drank any of the 'wishy-washy' French wines; he only drank 'real wine', which then was considered to be Port or Madeira. This preference obviously originated during the Napoleonic wars.

In fact, the truth of the matter is that any man who habitually consumes excess alcohol, whatever the form, has a raised uric acid. This level may be raised by any further insult to the body such as a night out or an extra good meal. Similarly, excesses in the other direction — in other words an extremely stringent dieting régime — can lead to the same problems.

The reason for excess leading to an attack of gout is probably that the lactic acid in the body rises with dietary excess. This in turn blocks the excretion of uric acid by the kidneys. The level of uric acid in the body rises and the excess is deposited in the joints — leading eventually to pain, swelling and all the symptoms of a classical attack.

The first attack of gout is a most alarming event. Often during the early forties, and in the middle of the night, there is a sudden agonising pain in one joint. Most probably a joint that has been subjected to repeated minor damage over many years. This explains why the big toe is the most susceptible. Other commonly affected joints are wrists, ankles and knees.

The joint will be swollen and exquisitely painful. Over the joint, the skin is swollen, red and shiny. The pain is made worse by any movement. Often the disease is accompanied by a general debilitating illness. Not unnaturally, or surprisingly, the patient is fractious and irritable!

Even without treatment, the attack will pass off in a few days, although it is kinder, not only to the patient, but also to his family, to treat it with one of the modern drugs that lower the uric acid level in the body; and also to use an anti-inflamatory drug.

The condition tends to recur, although at no specified or regular interval. Indeed, there may be a mercifully long gap of many years between attacks.

Whether long-term treatment is required is a matter dependant on the condition of the patient and the results of tests that are carried out. It is, nonetheless, a good idea to impose some dietary restrictions in order to prevent further attacks. To this end, some general principles can be laid down.

Firstly, in common with many conditions, the obese must lose weight and get down to the normal weight range for his or her height. This, in itself, actually helps reduce the uric acid in the body.

Crash diets, beloved of jockeys and film stars, are completely forbidden. To do this may actually increase the dangers of another attack of gout. Even after a short time, a diet like this can cause a rise in the uric acid level in the blood and, therefore, increase the risks of a further attack. Equally, feasting should be avoided.

Excess alcohol may be a causative factor in precipitating an attack and it is important to be honest with oneself when replying to questions about one's alcohol intake.

The basic tenet for anyone suffering from gout is that all alcohol should be restricted. It does not matter in what form it is taken — it must be limited. It is a scientific fact that, if you have more than two drinks per day regularly, your uric acid level will rise above normal. Therefore, it is reasonable to allow one drink per day, with the occasional second drink on celebrations and holidays. This will do much to reduce the frequency of attacks.

In order to avoid complications of gout like kidney stones, ensure a high fluid intake. Not, of course, based on alcohol!

There is no evidence to suggest that any particular wine or spirit is more likely to cause gout than another. Any alcohol can cause, and is just as likely to cause, gout as any other.

A common misconception is that the uric acid level in a wine plays a part in causing gout. Since no wine contains this acid, and it is in fact made during the metabolism of proteins, and is not made in the same way as the acids met with in winemaking, there is no danger of gout from the composition of a wine — merely its excessive consumption!

Likewise, the age of a wine has no effect on the chances of having an attack of gout, unless a particularly mellow wine is a greater incentive to drink excessively which will, as we have seen, increase the odds.

The alcoholic strength of a drink has no part to play in the development of gout.

As with all conditions requiring medical treatment, it is vital to discuss not only treatment but also whether you may drink. However, if permission is granted, there is no reason why a gout sufferer should not enjoy the occasional glass of wine, and run no risk of further attacks.

While gout is by no means the only disease affecting the joints, it is the most important to the winemaker and brewer in that the condition and alcohol have a direct causal relationship. Other joint diseases have no taboos in regard to alcohol except for the usual one about drugs and drink. Having said that, let us turn to wine ingredients and see if we can find some that can help either gout, or other arthritic processes.

Among the non poisonous plants used in the herbal treatment of arthritic conditions are the following:

MEDICINAL HERBS USED IN THE TREATMENT of ARTHRITIC CONDITIONS:

Birch, Silver	European Goldenrod
Blackcurrant	Juniper
Black Elder	Meadow Sweet
Burdock	Nettle
Comfrey	Parsley
Dandelion	Wormwood
European Centaury	

Any other plants mentioned as having herbal actions should not be used for winemaking as they have poisonous actions which makes them dangerous to ingest. As with any plant from which you might wish to make a wine — *if in doubt do not use it.*

Birch, Silver

See Chapter 7; page 61.

Birch Sap Wine

See Chapter 7; page 61.

Blackcurrant

See Chapter 7; page 62.

Blackcurrant Wine

See Chapter 7; page 62.

Black Elder

The use of the elder is as widespread in herbal treatments as it is universally used in winemaking. As we saw earlier, the elder was used to improve the quality of a poor *Port*.

The elder flower was used to make *Elderflower Water* — a much prized lotion for keeping the complexion clear and also for clearing spots. It was said to whiten the skin. Like the washing up liquid, it whitened and softened the hands if used when washing; the use of the flowers in the bath as a bath oil is considered (even today by at least one French doctor) to be a sovereign remedy against nervous conditions.

Elderflower Tea was widely used as part of the treatment of lung conditions since it aids the clearing of the bronchial tubes of phlegm. It was also used in the treatment of colds and sore throats since it soothes and also helps lower temperatures. Taken regularly, the tea was used as a tonic. Elderflower vinegar was an alternative formulation to treat throat and chest conditions.

The flowers were used to make a poultice to ease inflamatory conditions; which were also thought to be helped by the application of elderflower lotion.

Ointments, made from the flowers, were used for burns or hair dressings. The ointment was used during the First World War extensively to treat horses.

Finally, the elderflower had a considerable use in cooking as a flavouring agent.

The elderberry, too, has a multitude of uses. As early as Roman times, it was used as a hair dye; a use underlined by Culpepper who recommended elder berries dissolved in wine to dye hair black.

As a medicinal herb, the elderberry is used for treatment of rheumatic conditions. The range of uses varies from diuretic to aperient; from the treatment of syphilis to epilepsy or piles.

As with the flowers, the berries have a wide use in the kitchen; for wines, jellies, vinegars, and preserves.

The pharmacopoeia of 1890 lists elder flowers as a perfume and a pleasant flavouring agent for medicines. There is no medicinal use given.

More recently, the pharmacopoeia lists the flowers as being useful as a vehicle for eye-lotions and as a skin lotion. Its use, as mentioned above, as a pomade or cosmetic ointment is still given. No mention is made in official pharmacopoeia of the berry.

Elderberry Wine

See Chapter 3; page 25.

Burdock

See Chapter 7; page 64.

Burdock Wine

See Chapter 7; page 64.

Centaury

A plant which appears to be of use in almost all medical conditions. It is particularly recommended as a bitter tonic and for kidney or liver problems. It was commonly used as Centaury Tea — an infusion of the dried plant — for muscular rheumatism; as well as a tonic. Although no longer in the British Pharmacopoeia, it is still in the pharmacopoeia of many countries — linked with other species of *Gentian,* a well known, and much used, stimulant of the appetite.

* **Centaury Wine**

Ingredient	Quantity per gallon	Quantity per 5 litres
Centaury plant	1 lb 4 oz	600 gms
Dates	8 oz	250 gms
Sugar	to SG 70	to SG 70
Yeast		
Vitamin B_1	6 mg	6 mg
Water	to volume	to volume

For the recommended additives, see Page 53.

Place the chopped Centaury in 4 pints (2 litres) water; bring up to boiling point and simmer for a few minutes before leaving to infuse for three hours. Strain off the herbs and add the other ingredients; first stoning and chopping the dates. When cool, add an active yeast starter.

Ferment on the pulp for four days. Rack into a demijohn, make to volume, and ferment to dryness under air lock. Rack and mature as usual. Sweeten to taste as described in Chapter 5.

Comfrey

This plant's country names give more than a clue to its herbal uses: *Boneset, Bruisewort,* and *Knitbone.* From these it is not difficult to realise the great store set by this plant as a healer of sprains, strains, and even helping to heal fractured bones. In addition, it is used to speed the healing of persistent ulcers.

Used as an internal medicine, its uses include the treatment of stomach ulcers, and also in the treatment of bronchitis.

*   **Comfrey Wine**

Ingredient	Quantity per gallon	Quantity per 5 litres
Comfrey Roots	5	5
Tannin	$\frac{1}{15}$ oz	2 gms
Apples	2 lbs	900 gms
Sugar	to SG 70	to SG 70
Citric Acid	$\frac{1}{3}$ oz	10 gms
Oranges	2	2
Yeast		
Vitamin B$_1$	6 mg	6 mg
Water	to volume	to volume

For the recommended additives, see Page 53.

If you prefer, use 2 lemons in place of the citric acid. Similarly, strong tea can be used instead of the tannin.

Having dug up the plant roots, clean them carefully, peel and chop into pieces. Boil in water until soft. Remove the scum that forms on the tops of the saucepan. Strain the water onto the sugar and add the oranges, sugar, and acid (or lemons). When cool, add an active yeast starter and the nutrients. Ferment for five days before straining into a demijohn; make to volume, and continue to dryness under air lock.

Rack and mature as usual. Sweeten to taste as described in Chapter 5.

Goldenrod

A plant that is *astringent* (i.e. it coats the surface of many organs and acts to protect it). It removes excess fluid from the body, and is said to be useful in the treatment of bladder stones. It is also known as *Woundwort* as a tribute to its action in healing persistent ulcers. It does not, nor does it seem to have been, in the pharmacopoeia.

✳ # Golden Rod Wine

Ingredient	Quantity per gallon	Quantity per 5 litres
Golden Rod petals	2 handsful	2 handsful
White grape concentrate	$\frac{1}{2}$ pint	250 mls
Sugar	to SG 70	to SG 70
Yeast	Champagne or Hock	
Vitamin B_1	6 mg	6 mg
Water	to volume	to volume

For the recommended additives, see Page 53.

Place the flowers in a plastic bucket with the grape concentrate and any permitted sugar. Add six pints of cold water. Mix thoroughly. Sterilise the must with one Campden tablet; cover and leave for twenty four hours. After this time, add an active yeast starter. Ferment on the flowers for four days. Then strain off the flowers, make to volume, and finish fermentation under air lock. The wine tends to have a persistent and unpleasant flavour when young. It therefore requires maturing for at least one year — perferably two.

Sweeten to taste as described in Chapter 5.

Gooseberry

Neither mentioned in later herbals, nor in the pharmacopoeia. However, historically, gooseberry leaves were considered a preventative of kidney stones. They were also used in teenage girls to establish their cycles. A more fanciful use of the berry was to eat is as prophylaxis against the plague. Gooseberry jelly was used as a convalescent food for liver sufferers.

Gooseberry Wine

See Chapter 3; page 23.

Juniper

The berry of this shrub is used in the making of Gin. Herbally, the berries have a wide range of uses, from soothing indigestion to kidney and bladder problems. It has been used in an ointment for the treatment of animals with chronic sores.

The major herbal use is as a diuretic in heart disease, but it is also used in the treatment of gout. The old pharmacopoeia listed its medicinal uses as being the same as the herbal values; and it retains its listing.

This plant should not be ingested during pregnancy. Nor should it be taken in the presence of kidney disease. This last *caveat* removes two of its main uses. For it is dangerous to assume the lack of kidney disease in the presence of excess body fluid; and gout sufferers are more prone to kidney disease than the normal population.

In view of this, although I give a recipe for juniper wine, it is not recommended wine to make. I give it more as a curio than anything else.

★ Juniper Wine

Ingredient	Quantity per gallon	Quantity per 5 litres
Juniper berries	3 lbs	1.5 kg
Raisins	1 lb	500 gms
Sugar	to SG 70	to SG 70
Yeast		
Vitamin B_1	6 mg	6 mg
Water	to volume	to volume

For the recommended additives, see Page 53.

Boil the berries in water for about three quarters of an hour. Strain off the liquid and, having washed and chopped the raisins, place all the ingredients and nutrients in a bucket. When cool, add an active yeast starter. Ferment on the pulp for one week. Then strain, make to volume, and finish fermentation to dryness under air lock.

Rack and mature. Sweeten to taste as described in Chapter 5.

Meadowsweet

See Chapter 7; page 67.

Meadowsweet Wine

See Chapter 7; page 67.

Nettle

See Chapter 7; page 68.

Nettle Wine

See Chapter 7; page 68.

Parsley

Apart from its wide use in cooking, parsley has many herbal uses. One preparation from the plant was used in the treatment of malaria and febrile illnesses. *Parsley Tea* was used in the First World War as an adjunct to the treatment of dysentery. There are claims that parsley leaves can 'cure' cancers. A claim that must be viewed with the gravest misgivings.

It is used for removal of excess fluid and in the treatment of kidney and other stones. On the basis that diuretics are good for many conditions, parsley is used herbally for rheumatic conditions. Again, not a commonly held medical view.

That parsley has a high iron content is indisputable; hence, it may help in the treatment of anaemia.

Apiol, the oil obtained from the herb, is listed in the pharmacopoeia. It is said to be of benefit for menstrual problems. But, it continues, it is of doubtful therapeutic value. Not only that, but it is poisonous to the kidneys; and so should not be taken in large quantities.

✶   **Parsley Wine**

Ingredient	Quantity per gallon	Quantity per 5 litres
Fresh parsley	1 lb	450 gms
Sugar	to SG 70	to SG 70
Ginger	1 medium root	1 medium root
Lemons	2	2
Tannin	⅙th oz	5 gms
Vitamin B$_1$	6 mg	6 mg
Water	to volume	to volume

For the recommended additives, see Page 53.

Wash the parsley, then boil until tender. Strain into a bucket and add the ginger, sugar and sliced lemons. Mix thoroughly. When cool, add an active yeast starter. Ferment on the pulp for two weeks. Then strain, make to volume, and ferment to dryness under air lock. Rack and mature in the usual way. Sweeten to taste as described in Chapter 5.

Wormwood

Also known as *Absinthe,* this is the plant from which the now illegal French drink Absinthe was made. It is highly toxic in high doses and P. C. Wren wrote many Foreign Legion stories around the effects it can have. It is one of the bitterest plants known to man, and was used at one time in the flavouring of beers. Wormwood tea has been used for depression (the plant can cause hallucinations; and like many drugs of addiction, gives the impression of being an anti-depressant). It has been used for indigestion and for the treatment of intestinal worms.

The old pharmacopoeia list its uses as a tonic and vermifuge, as well as mentioning its use in drink. It then states that 'its excessive use causes symptoms known as Absinthism'. The symptoms are restlessness, vomiting, vertigo, tremors, and convulsions. It is no longer in the pharmacopoeia.

The recipe that follows is not recommended for 'drinking', but, rather as a tonic wine; and to be taken as such — in small quantities.

✳ **Wormwood Wine**

Ingredient	Quantity per gallon	Quantity per 5 litres
Wormwood	4 oz	125 gms
Raisins	1 lb	500 gms
Rhubarb	1 lb	500 gms
Sugar	to SG 70	to SG 70
Vitamin B_1	6 mg	6 mg
Water	to volume	to volume

For the recommended additives, see Page 53.

Wash, peel and chop the rhubarb and raisins. Then boil for three quarters of an hour. Place in a bucket, add the sugar and mix thoroughly. When cool, add the nutrients and an active yeast starter. Ferment on the pulp for one week. Then strain, make to volume, and ferment to dryness under air lock. Rack and mature in the usual way. Sweeten to taste as described in Chapter 5.

The following are among the plants mentioned in the herbals as treatments for gout and other joint conditions that are toxic, and are not to be used for winemaking:

Aconite	Feverfew	Pokeweed
Alder Buckthorn	Garden Violet	Poke Root
Alfafa	Gotu Kola	Red Bryony
Bittersweet	Heartsease	Restharrow
Black Cohosh	Horse Radish	St. Benedict Thistle
Black Poplar	Jamaica Dogwood	Sassafras
Buck Bean	Kava Kava	Shave Grass
Buttercup	Lady's Thumb	White Melilot
Bryony, White	Life Everlasting	Willow
Cayenne	Lignum Vitae	Wintergreen
Chickweed	Marsh Tea	Witch Grass
Devil's Claw	Meadow Saffron	Yellow Melilot
Dropwort	Monks Hood	Yew
European Aspen	Mountain Holly	

9 A Little Wine for Thy Stomach's Sake

All foods, with the exception of sugars and alcohol, need to be at least partially digested before being taken from the intestine into the body. Except for glucose, no food is absorbed until it reaches the small intestine — except alcohol which is absorbed unchanged from the stomach. If alcohol were not absorbed directly from the stomach, the pre-dinner aperitif would have to be drunk at teatime to have its expected ice-breaking effect! While some alcohol is absorbed directly from the lining of the mouth and lungs, it is minute in quantity.

Because alcohol is absorbed directly, and unchanged, from the stomach and small intestine, a good meal before drinking can help slow down (but not prevent), drunkenness by 'diluting' the drink.

As well as for the social (or rather anti-social) effects, it is safer on medical grounds not to drink on an empty stomach. One reason is that alcohol is an irritant to the stomach and can cause serious upset.

Alcohol is an irritant to the intestinal tract, and, as would be expected, the stronger the drink the greater the irritation. In severe cases of gastric (or stomach) irritation bleeding can occur. This is caused by the alcohol precipitating the protein in the stomach lining. Pain may result from this protein destruction which may, in turn, lead to exposure of the gastric nerves. Blood vessels thus exposed to the acid in the stomach, as well as the alcohol in the drink, are then eroded and may bleed. In addition alcohol causes blood vessels to dilate. As a result the blood vessel walls (especially the veins) become thinner and more likely to burst; rather like an over inflated balloon. Add the greater blood flow caused by alcohol to this list of troubles and you can see that alcohol in excess can cause fatal haemorrhage.

When we examine the actions of alcohol on the brain, we shall see how it can cause vomiting. If there is blood inside the stomach this too can have the same effect. Thus, after a 'good night out', there can be worrying, not to say severe, vomiting of blood. This causes further damage to the gastric vessels, so that alcoholic gastritis can take some time to settle down.

The alcoholic or 'morning-after' sufferer who partakes in the 'Hair of the Dog' or has a prairie oyster is not likely to help his stomach recover. Paradoxically, however, he may feel better in himself — at least until further vomiting occurs. While on the subject of 'hangover cures', *avoid any product containing aspirin.* This is a drug which is irritant to the stomach and can lead to bleeding.

Sensibly, most of us do not drink sufficient quantities of alcohol to reach this state of affairs; for should this insult be continually repeated the stomach may become scarred. It may shrink; and the gastric walls become so thin that an artery in an affected area may be eroded so that there may be a massive, possibly fatal, haemorrhage.

Following excess alcohol there is usually an aversion to food because excess alcohol stops the flow of gastric juices. Since appetite is, in part, due to the stimulation of the juices, their continued inhibition explains in part why the alcoholic does not eat properly.

However, on the brighter side, who does not enjoy an aperitif? In small amounts, and in not too great a concentration, alcohol stimulates the appetite. This effect is greatest with beers and vermouths because the *Quassia* used as a heading liquid in some beers, and *Gentian* in the latter are two of the best appetite stimulants known.

Two well known advertising slogans tell us that their stout is 'good for you' and 'do you good'. Surprisingly, these statements are true. Not only with regard to appetite, but also, since they are bottle matured, they contain yeast and, hence, a small amount of vitamin B and other vitamins. There is a minute amount of iron — not as much as we are led to believe, but iron nonetheless.

Normally in the course of a day, we eat about 20 milligrammes of iron. By contrast, a pint of stout contains only 0.25 mgm of iron. However, iron does sometimes act, in some way, as a tonic. Scientifically, however, this should be almost insignificant.

Perhaps better than a stout for the convalescent is a naturally made sweet wine. Not only does it contain more calories (about 80 per 100 mls) but the iron content can be as high as 1.2 mgm per 100 mls. Obviously, this last suggestion cannot apply to the diabetic who has to exclude free sugar from his diet.

The advantage of wine over beer in dietary terms is that, having had a drink before or with a meal, more food is taken. This is obviously better than 'eating' alcohol alone.

With regard to vitamin content, wine comes out slightly ahead of beer. Both contain roughly the same amount of vitamin B. Wine on the other hand has more folic acid — an important requirement for making blood. Spirits, on the other hand, contain no vitamins. A situation which can prove disastrous to the alcoholic.

Again, white wines are probably better for both the convalescent patient and heavy drinker. Although the tannins in red wines may confer some protection on the stomach lining against the irritation of alcohol, they combine with food protein not the gut lining, so that protection is not available further down the intestinal tract.

The colouring matter of red wines is chiefly derived from acid anthocyanins. They belong to a family of chemicals known as glucosides and are formed of glucose with other elements attached. Since all glucosides are irritants they can irritate the stomach. To compound this problem their action on the brain and heart can lead to vomiting and diarrhoea, and itching of the skin.

Finally, in this chapter, a few words on allergy to wines.

Allergy is due to the secretion of a chemical by the body called *5-hydroxytryptamine* (or, thankfully, 5HT, for short). It is present in everybody, but usually kept under control by enzymes. If this chemical is present in any food we eat, and it is either too much for the body to cope with, or the eater is lacking in the enzymes necessary, an allergic reaction may occur.

Substances liable to cause allergic reactions are present in both red fruit and their juices. One chemical, *catechol,* is present in tannin. Another, *Proline* is an amino-acid. Eating these substances usually results in their being broken down in the gut. On the other hand, in fermentation, tryptophan may be synthesised. This may be broken down in the liver to 5HT and so may cause an allergic reaction. Tryptophan is also broken down by *Pyridoxine,* (vitamin B_6).

If this is lacking (and this is not uncommon in ladies), the chances of an allergic reaction will be increased.

White wines contain very small amounts of tannin, and so are less likely to cause this problem of allergy.

Typically, a reaction to wine will cause a generalised blushing; possibly developing into a rash. Usually, there will be an increase in nasal and tear secretion; as well as the possibility of a puffiness around the eyes.

Luckily these reactions are extremely rare and, by avoiding a wine known to cause such problems, 'curable'. If, however, red wines do upset you, and you still wish to make them, the following suggestions *might* overcome this sad state of affairs. Firstly, use either a very short pulp fermentation time — although a juice extraction method will probably be better. The use of vitamin B_6 tablets in the must will help prevent tryptophan production.

Unfortunately, no-one can ever guarantee the success of such schemes. If this fails, there is only one solution: eschew entirely those wines which cause these reactions.

Agrimony

Used herbally for the treatment of intestinal infections or gall bladder problems. In addition, it is used for some urinary conditions. It has not been listed in the pharmacopoeia.

∗   Agrimony Wine

Ingredient	Quantity per gallon	Quantity per 5 litres
Fresh Agrimony	1 lb	500 gms
White grape concentrate	½ pint	250 mls
Sugar	to SG 70	to SG 70
Yeast	Champagne, Hock or Bordeaux	
Vitamin B_1	6 mg	6 mg
Water	to volume	to volume

For the recommended additives, see Page 53.

Method as for *Golden Rod Wine.* See Chapter 8; page 79. This wine is one which is probably best sweetened (as described in Chapter 5).

Angelica

Best known to most people as the green decorative strips on cakes and confectionery. It is recommended herbally for delicate digestions — it is particularly used as an appetite stimulant. Other uses include asthma and other chest conditions. It was first included in the pharmacopoeia in 1934 and used as a treatment for fevers and as a tonic.

★ Angelica Wine

Ingredient	Quantity per gallon	Quantity per 5 litres
Angelica leaves	½ lb	500 gms
Candied cherries	½ lb	500 gms
Candied lemon peel	½ lb	500 gms
Sugar	to SG 70	to SG 70
Yeast		
Vitamin B$_1$	6 mg	6 mg
Water	to volume	to volume

For the recommended additives, see Page 53.

Chop the candied fruit and wash the leaves. Then boil together for twenty minutes in about two pints (1 litre) water. Allow to cool. Add the nutrients and an active yeast starter. Strain into a fermentation jar with air lock and make to volume. Check the SG and add sugar to SG 70. Ferment to dryness. Rack and mature in the usual manner. Sweeten to taste as described in Chapter 5.

✳   # Angelica Liqueur

Ingredient	Quantity per 2 pints	Quantity per 1 litre
Angelica Stem	1 oz	30 gms
Boiled bitter almond	1 oz	30 gms
Brandy	1 pint	500 mls
Water	to volume	to volume

Place the angelica and almonds in the brandy and allow to steep for one week. Strain off the fruit. It is probably best to sweeten the liqueur, although since free sugar is being avoided, the finished product will be somewhat 'thin'. If you wish to 'break the rules', then make a syrup with 2 lbs (1 kg) of sugar dissolved in half a pint of water and blend the brandy and syrup. Allow to mature for several months. If making the syrup version, do not forget to make allowances for the sugar in your diet.

Aniseed

Although the chief herbal use is in chest conditions, it is also used as a gastric sedative — especially for colic and wind. These uses are quoted in the old pharmacopoeia, as is its use in preventing colic due to laxative medicines. The herb still maintains its place.

✳   # Aniseed Aperitif

Ingredient	Quantity per bottle	Quantity per bottle
140° Spirit	13 oz	390 mls
Sugar	10 oz	300 gms
Aniseed essence	1 bottle	1 bottle

Make the sugar into a syrup with 5 oz (150 mls) water. When cool, mix the ingredients together. As with the previous liqueur, the free sugar needs to be allowed for if you take this drink.

89

Apple

Well matured apple wine was recommended by Galen as a cure for all ills. Eaten either stewed or grated, apple flesh does help settle an attack of diarrhoea. (Other than foods like *Arrowroot* the patient should starve for at least one day). The pectin, together with the tannin in the apple, presumably coats the intestinal wall and soothes it. On the other hand, apple skins are a mild laxative and have been used, dried, to make a tea, in the relief of rheumatic conditions. The acid in apples, *Malic Acid,* is a good tooth cleaning agent. The pharmacopoeia still refers to proprietary preparations containing this as a dentifrice when it is 'not convenient to use a tooth brush'.

Apple Wine

See Chapter 3; page 17.

Artichoke

The leaves of the *Jerusalem Artichoke* are possibly toxic. It is, therefore, important not to use this part of the plant for wine-making. Herbally, the plant is used in the treatment of gall bladder and liver disease, and also for some kidney conditions. The leaves of the *Globe Artichoke* are mentioned in the pharmacopoeia as *possibly* having diuretic properties and being of benefit in gall bladder disease.

✳ Artichoke Wine

Ingredient	Quantity per gallon	Quantity per 5 litres
Artichoke tubers	4 lbs	1.8 kg
Orange	1	1
Lemon	1	1
Raisins	½ lb	500 gms
Sugar	to SG 70	to SG 70
Tannin	$\frac{1}{30}$th oz	1 gm
Yeast	Sherry	Sherry
Vitamin B_1	6 mg	6 mg
Water	to volume	to volume

For the recommended additives, see Page 53.

Slice the artichokes and place in 4 pints (2 litres) water. Add the zest of the orange and lemon. Wash and chop the raisins before adding them. Boil for half an hour. The juice of the lemon and orange, and any permitted sugar, is added together with the tannin. (If you prefer, use one cup of strong tea in place of the tannin). Allow to cool before adding the nutrients and an active yeast starter. Ferment on the pulp for two days and then strain off, make to volume, and ferment to dryness under air lock. Rack, mature, and sweeten as usual.

Burdock

See Chapter 7; page 64.

Burdock Wine

See Chapter 7; page 64.

Burnet

Used herbally for diarrhoea, it is also considered to be a tonic. It has been used as a flavouring for herb beers. The tincture is listed in the pharmacopoeia as a 'carminative' or an intestinal soothing preparation.

✶ Burnet Wine

Ingredient	Quantity per gallon	Quantity per 5 litres
Burnet	2 lbs	1 kg
White grape concentrate	½ pint	500 mls
Sugar	to SG 70	to SG 70
Yeast		
Vitamin B$_1$	6 mg	6 mg
Water	to volume	to volume

For the recommended additives, see Page 53.

Wash, chop and then boil the Burnet for about ten minutes. Strain the liquid into a fermentation jar and add the grape concentrate and any permitted sugar. When cool add the nutrients and an active yeast starter. When the fermentation dies down, make to volume and then ferment under air lock to dryness. Rack and mature in the usual way. Sweeten to taste as described in Chapter 5.

Celery

Its reputation as a sedative is considered doubtful by the pharmacopoeia. The herbal uses for rheumatism and for relief of colic are mentioned. Herbally, it is also used by nursing mothers.

✳ Celery Wine

Ingredient	Quantity per gallon	Quantity per 5 litres
Celery	4 lbs	2 kgs
Sugar	to SG 70	to SG 70
Citric acid	1 teaspoon	5 gms
Vitamin B_1	6 mg	6 mg
Water	to volume	to volume

For the recommended additives, see Page 53.

Wash and chop the celery. Boil until tender (the celery can be used for lunch). Strain the liquid over the sugar. When cool add the nutrients, lemon juice and an active yeast starter. When fermentation dies down, make to volume and ferment to dryness under air lock. Rack and mature in the usual way. Sweeten to taste as described in Chapter 5.

Centaury

See Chapter 8; page 76.

Centaury Wine

See Chapter 8; page 77.

Chamomile

This herb is well known to most in the form of *Chamomile Tea* — a relaxing and soothing beverage. Its major use is as a tranquiliser, including digestive upsets. It is also used in chest conditions and in the treatment of fevers. The pharmacopoeia points out that in large doses it causes vomiting. A powder prepared from the plant is used in some shampoos.

✳ Chamomile Wine

Ingredient	Quantity per gallon	Quantity per 5 litres
Chamomile	1 head	1 head
Raisins	1 lb	500 gms
Sugar	to SG 70	to SG 70
Tannin	$\frac{1}{2}$ teaspoon	2 gms
Citric acid	1 teaspoon	5 gms
Yeast		
Vitamin B_1	6 mg	6 mg
Water	to volume	to volume

For the recommended additives, see Page 53.

Remove all the 'green bits' and pour 6 pints (3 litres) boiling water over the flowers. Add the chopped raisins and sugar. When cool add the nutrients and an active yeast starter. Ferment on the pulp for five days; then rack, make to volume, and finish fermenting to dryness under air lock. Rack and mature in the usual way. Sweeten to taste as described in Chapter 5.

Comfrey

See Chapter 8; page 77.

Comfrey Wine

See Chapter 8; page 78.

Crab Apple

See above under *Apple.* Page 90.

Crab Apple Wine

See Chapter 3; page 18.

Dandelion

See Chapter 7; page 64.

Dandelion Wine

See Chapter 7; page 65.

Dill

A herb that is widely used for wind and colic. It is added to laxatives to prevent pain. Both these uses are listed in the pharmacopoeia, as well as its use as a flavouring for childrens' medicines.

*　Dill Wine

Ingredient	Quantity per gallon	Quantity per 5 litres
Fresh Dill	1 lb	500 gms
Sugar	to SG 70	to SG 70
Tannin	$\frac{1}{2}$ teaspoon	2.5 gms
Citric acid	1 teaspoon	5 gms
Vitamin B_1	6 mg	6 mg
Water	to volume	to volume

For the recommended additives, see Page 53.

If you prefer, use $1\frac{1}{2}$-2 oz (45-60 gms) of the dried herb. Wash and chop the herb. Boil in 4 pints (2 litres) water for 5-10 minutes. Add the sugar and mix well. Allow to cool, add the nutrients and an active yeast starter. When fermentation has died down, make to volume and ferment to dryness under air lock. Rack and mature in the usual way. Sweeten to taste.

Elecampane

See Chapter 12; page 126.

Elecampane Wine

See Chapter 12; page 126.

Fennel

A well known kitchen herb, the plant is used herbally for almost any digestive or bowel problem. Additionally, it is the basis for an eyewash and gargle, and helps nursing mothers. It has always figured in the pharmacopoeia for its bowel soothing properties, and is, today, enjoying something of a 'comeback' as a pleasant infants' drink which acts like gripe water — but with none of the latter's drawbacks.

* Fennel Wine

Ingredient	Quantity per gallon	Quantity per 5 litres
Young Fennel	$\frac{1}{2}$ lb	250 gms
Raisins	1 lb	500 gms
Sugar	to SG 70	to SG 70
Vitamin B_1	6 mg	6 mg
Water	to volume	to volume

For the recommended additives, see Page 53.

Wash and chop both the raisins and the fennel, then boil in 4 pints (2 litres) water for twenty minutes. Strain. Add any permitted sugar and mix well. When cool, add nutrients and an active yeast starter. When fermentation has died down, make to volume, and ferment under air lock to dryness. Rack, mature and sweeten as usual.

Ginger

See Chapter 7; page 65.

Ginger Wine

See Chapter 7; page 66.

Hops

Listed in the pharmacopoeia for their use as appetite stimulants. The hop is used as a herbal sleeping draught and tranquiliser. A pillow stuffed with hops is said to induce a restful night. An old use was in the treatment of alcoholism. Many of these old medical uses are still applicable herbally.

✱ Hop Wine

Ingredient	Quantity per gallon	Quantity per 5 litres
Hops	3 oz	75 gms
Ginger	1 oz	25 gms
Orange	1	1
Lemon	1	1
Sugar	to SG 70	to SG 70
Yeast		
Vitamin B$_1$	6 mg	6 mg
Water	to volume	to volume

For the recommended additives, see Page 53.

Chop the ginger and boil with the hops for one hour. Strain over the sugar and add the juice from the orange and lemon. When cool add the nutrients and an active yeast starter. When fermentation has died down, make to volume, and ferment under air lock to dryness. Rack and mature in the usual way. Sweeten to taste as described in Chapter 5.

Juniper

See Chapter 8; page 80.

Juniper Wine

See Chapter 8; page 80.

Lemon Balm

Otherwise known as *Balm,* this herb appears in many phar-macopoeia for its soothing action on the digestion. It is possible that the herb can protect against viral infections. In addition to these actions, it is used as a herbal tranquiliser.

✶ Lemon Balm Wine

Ingredient	Quantity per gallon	Quantity per 5 litres
Balm leaves	2 pints	1 litre
White grape concentrate	1 pint	500 mls
Sugar	to SG 70	to SG 70
Yeast		
Vitamin B_1	6 mg	6 mg
Water	to volume	to volume

For the recommended additives, see Page 53.

Method as for *Dandelion Wine.* See Chapter 8; page 65.

Lovage

In addition to its use in soothing the digestion and stimu-lating the appetite, lovage is used in chest complaints. It has never appeared in the official pharmacopoeia.

*   **Lovage Wine**

Ingredient	Quantity per gallon	Quantity per 5 litres
Lovage leaves	2 lbs	1 kg
White grape concentrate	½ pint	500 mls
Sugar	to SG 70	to SG 70
Yeast		
Vitamin B$_1$	6 mg	6 mg
Water	to volume	to volume

For the recommended additives, see Page 53.

Wash and chop the lovage. Boil in 4 pints (2 litres) water for quarter of an hour. Strain off the liquid. Add the grape concentrate and permitted sugar. Mix thoroughly. When cool add the nutrients and an active yeast starter. When fermentation has died down, make to volume, and ferment to dryness under air lock. Rack and mature in the usual way. Sweeten to taste as described in Chapter 5.

Marigold

Used herbally as a healing agent for such conditions as gastric ulcers, mouth ulcers, and varicose ulcers. It is also used as an anti-infective agent. According to the pharmacopoeia all these actions are doubtful. It does, however, concede that the flowers are useful as an 'aromatic'.

*   **Marigold Wine**

Ingredient	Quantity per gallon	Quantity per 5 litres
Marigold flowers	6 pints	3 litres
Sugar	to SG 70	to SG 70
Lemons	2	2
Vitamin B$_1$	6 mg	6 mg
Water	to volume	to volume

 For the recommended additives, see Page 53.

Dissolve the sugar in hot water. When cool, crush the flowers (making sure that only the flower heads are used), and add them to the syrup. Add the juice and zest of the lemons, nutrients and an active yeast starter. Ferment the flowers for one week. Stir twice daily to break up the cap that develops on the surface. Strain into a demijohn, make to volume, and ferment to dryness under air lock. Rack and mature in the usual way. Sweeten to taste as described in Chapter 5.

Allow this wine to mature for at least six or nine months before drinking.

Meadowsweet

See Chapter 7; page 67.

Meadowsweet Wine

See Chapter 7; page 67.

Parsley

See Chapter 8; page 81.

Parsley Wine

See Chapter 8; page 82.

Plum

Both the fresh and dried fruit — the latter are, of course, *Prunes,* and well known for their laxative actions. They are also said to aid digestion. Prunes are listed in the old pharmocopoeia as being of nutritional value, as well as refrigerants, (something that quenches the thirst and reduces the body's heat). The laxative action of prunes ensures that they are still listed.

Plum Wine

See Chapter 3; page 22.

Quince

Because of its high tannin content, quince has a soothing action on the stomach. The pharmacopoeia still lists the seed as a mucilage and as the base for some creams and lotions. In Roman times, Pliny considered it a cardinal spell for warding off the evil eye. Its main use is in cooking and winemaking.

Quince Wine

See Chapter 3; page 18.

Rhubarb

The root is used herbally as a laxative. In small doses, it is useful in the treatment of colic. The plant has the longest entry in the pharmacopoeia of all the herbs mentioned in this book. There are a wide range of commercial preparations made with rhubarb root — all laxatives. Apart from chronic constipation, rhubarb is considered one of the better laxatives because the natural tannin helps to soothe the gut as well as help the primary condition.

Rhubarb Wine

See Chapter 3; page 19.

Sage

Used as an appetite stimulant in convalescence, sage is also used as the base for a mouth wash and gargle in throat and mouth conditions and infections. It has a use in treating excess sweating. The pharmacopoeia says that it has *carminative* properties (it eases wind and colic) and that it may have the other properties mentioned here.

 This herb must not be used during pregnancy.

* **Sage Wine**

Ingredient	Quantity per gallon	Quantity per 5 litres
Sage leaves	2 lbs	1 kg
Raisins	1 lb	500 gms
Barley	$\frac{1}{2}$ lb	250 gms
Lemons	2	2
Sugar	to SG 70	to SG 70
Yeast		
Vitamin B$_1$	6 mg	6 mg
Water	to volume	to volume

For the recommended additives, see Page 53.

Wash and chop the raisins. Pour 4 pints (2 litres) boiling water over them, and add the barley and sage leaves — washed and chopped. When the mixture has cooled, add the juice of the lemons, nutrients, and an active yeast starter. Ferment on the pulp for one week, stirring twice daily. Rack, make to volume, and ferment to dryness under air lock. Rack and mature in the usual manner. Sweeten to taste.

Thyme

A tranquilising herb that soothes coughs and other chest conditions by this action. It is also used for relieving wind and colic, and has an anti-infective role in mouth and throat conditions. An extract still used today as a medical mouthwash is *Thymol* obtained from the thyme plant. According to the old pharmacopoeia, this is a better arrester of fermentation than carbolic acid. Recent pharmacopoeiae recommend Thymol for whooping cough and bronchitis, as well as for external use as a rub for rheumatics.

✳   Thyme Wine

Ingredient	Quantity per gallon	Quantity per 5 litres
Thyme leaves and flowers	1 pint	500 mls
White grape concentrate	½ pint	250 mls
Sugar	to SG 70	to SG 70
Citric acid	2 teaspoons	10 gms
Tannin	½ teaspoon	2.5 gms
Yeast		
Vitamin B$_1$	6 mg	6 mg
Water	to volume	to volume

For the recommended additives, see Page 53.

Rinse and wash the thyme, pour 6 pints (3 litres) boiling water over the leaves. When cool, add 2 Campden tablets, cover and leave for twenty four hours. Stir several times. Strain off the liquid and add the rest of the ingredients. Mix thoroughly, and add an active yeast starter. When fermentation has died down, make to volume. Ferment under air lock to dryness. Rack and mature as usual. Sweeten to taste as described in Chapter 5.

Wormwood

See Chapter 8; page 82.

Wormwood Wine

See Chapter 8; page 83.

The following herbs and plants are listed in herbal books as having beneficial actions on the digestive system. As they all contain suspicious ingredients, and in many cases are frankly toxic, they should not be used for winemaking.

Alder Blackthorn	Horse Chestnut	Oak Bark
Blue Flag	Horseradish	Tansy
Bryony	Lucerne	Tormentil
Celandine	Milk Thistle	Wild Lettuce
Henbane	Nightshade	

This is not a comprehensive list, but does encompass the most poisonous species listed in the books. As always, if in doubt, *do not use the plant for winemaking.*

10 Alcohol as Food

There can be no doubt as to the place that alcohol can occupy in dietary terms. The best way of looking at this is to examine some of the chemistry involved. To start, let us look at the way in which alcohol is metabolised, or broken down, in the body. Logically, the starting point is to examine the composition of a typical wine must and beer wort.

TABLE 6

I Non-Volatile Constituents of Wine:

(a) Sugars: Glucose, Fructose, Pentose, Sucrose
(b) Non Sugar Constituents:
    (i) Combustible: Starch, Protein, Pectin, Cellulose, Acids, Tannin, Colouring, Vitamins.
    (ii) Non Combustible: Potassium, Sodium, Calcium, Magnesium, Iron, Manganese, Phosphorus, Iodine, Sulphur.

II Volatile Constituents:

Alcohol, Esters, Volatile Acids, Aldehydes. (All present in trace quantities).

Alternatively, this can be expressed quantitively as totals of the main groups of constituents.

TABLE 7

Quantitive Constituents of Wine:

Water	70-80%
Sugar	10-35%
Acid	0.03-0.04%
Minerals	0.02-0.04%
Nitrogen	0.05-0.01%

Quantitive Constituents of Beer:

Water	90%
Sugar	8%
Nitrogen	0.1%
Acid	
Non-Fermentable Sugars	

Thus, it can be seen that beer worts and whisky washings have, basically, the same composition as a wine must — but with the addition of dextrins (which are non-fermentable sugars), hops, and caramel.

During fermentation there is a rise and fall respectively in the alcohol and fermentable sugar content, otherwise, to all intents and purposes, the constitutents remain the same.

There are two sets of chemical reactions which take place. On the one hand, alcohol is made by fermentation, while, on the other, it is utilised in the body — as are many of the other constituents of 'drinks'. Without going into too much detail, suffice it to say that two impressive sounding series of reactions — known as *The Kreb's Cycle* and *Glycolysis* — are responsible for the changes that take place in the sugars.

These reactions produce alcohol, provided the conditions are correct. Firstly, there must be an absence of oxygen (in other words, *anaerobic fermentation).*

Once alcohol has been ingested it is absorbed into the blood stream. From here it passes through the liver where it is acted upon by an enzyme called *Alcohol Dehydrogenase* which turns the alcohol into a chemical known as an aldehyde. This in turn enters the Kreb's Cycle to break it down to its basic water and carbon dioxide.

As the body does not contain an unlimited amount of this enzyme (a chemical which speeds up a chemical reaction), it means that an excess intake of alcohol will lead to an over-loading of the system. This causes what one might call a traffic jam at the start of the process of breaking down alcohol.

Once a comparatively small amount of alcohol has been treated by the liver; the greater part will remain in the body and cause depression of the brain and nerves.

Other constituents of beverages are dealt with in much the same manner. Residual sugars in a sweet wine are metabolised in the pathways we have discussed above, with the exception of *pentoses*, (sugars with five carbon atoms in their makeup). One of these, *Ribose*, is important in helping the body make nucleic acids. These, in their turn, make up the chromosomes. Because these sugars are not metabolised in the same way as glucose, they have no adverse affects on the diabetic.

Acids present in the finished wine enter the body's metabolism in the Kreb's Cycle. So we can see that wine or beer, as ever in moderation, can help the body with its daily requirements.

Colouring matter in wines is mostly due to *anthocyanins* and *tannins*. They are mostly excreted through the gut, without being absorbed. This is especially true of tannins which, as we have already seen, combine with proteins to form insoluble compounds.

Vitamins in beers and wines are absorbed into the body and utilised as part of the body's essential needs. Similarly, metals are absorbed and put to good use.

Any excess water that the body absorbs from whatever source, will be excreted, or got rid of, from the body by the kidneys.

Thus, we can see that the utilisation of 'normal' amounts of beer or wine is a valuable source of small quantities of 'instant energy'. Do not, however, rely on alcohol for your basic diet. For a start, Table 8 shows just how widely divergent drink is from a balanced diet in regard to vitamins. To emphasise this, Table 9 shows the absence of important food stuffs (fats and proteins) from drinks.

Proteins are as important to the body as carbohydrate and it is vital to realise that all the alcohol in the world will not help in its manufacture to the extent required by your body.

Again, alcohol is deficient in fat and related compounds that can be made into fats. The importance of these compounds, no matter how much people value slim figures, is that they are a source of 'long term' energy to provide against lean times. It goes without saying that the presence of fat must not be to the extent of being 'fat'. One of the most important reasons of including at least some fat in our diets is to enable the body to absorb some of the vitamins which can only be passed into the blood stream if they are in fatty solution.

All of these substances essential to man are absent from alcoholic drinks, and since vitamins are not manufactured in the body, a source of supply is essential. Again this precludes alcohol from being the basis of a diet.

As far as the food value of plants used for winemaking is concerned, we have already seen the typical composition of a wine or beer. The main contribution to diet is the sugar and the calories they provide, fats, protein and vitamins being essentially absent from wines.

It may be of interest to note those plants used in winemaking that do have high concentrations of the different vitamins, although fermentation destroys most of them.

Vitamin A. Is essential for healthy skin, bones and teeth. It also plays a part in the making of red blood cells. Although vitamin A is not found in plants, its precursor, *carotene* is present in many winemaking ingredients. Some of this compound is found in the finished wine.

Some home made wine ingredients that contain carotene are: Dandelion, Carrots, Apricot, Turnip, Parsely, Nettle, Elderberry, Cranberry, Bilberry, Cowslip, Elecampane, Red Currant, Rowan.

The vitamin B group have varied functions in the body. Most are found in plants, but in finished wine or beer the amount present is small.

Vitamin B$_1$. This is essential in the production of energy by the body, as well as for the function of the nerves and heart. It is found in the following wine ingredients: Rice, Turnip, Barley, Dandelion, Raisin, Figs, Potato, Dates, Pineapple, Orange, Parsley.

Vitamin B$_2$. A vitamin necessary for cell growth and the utilisation of protein by the body. Again, it is only present in wines and beers in small amounts. Some ingredients in which it is found are: Brewer's Yeast, Turnip, Dandelion, Apricots, Dates, Figs, Raspberries, Barley, Parsnip.

Vitamin C.   (or Ascorbic acid) is present in large amounts in ripening fruit. It is entirely used up or destroyed during fermentation and maturation of wines and beers. In the human body, it is needed for many cell reactions and enables the body to make use of many nutrients. It is present in large quantities in Blackberries, Rose Hips, Parsley, Bilberries, Raspberries, and Rowan.

Vitamin D.   Like Vitamin A, this does not occur in plants. Its precursors, called *Sterols,* do. This Vitamin is necessary for bone and tooth growth and health. Yeast contains large amounts. Wines and beers contain no Vitamin D.

So, it is safe to say that no wine has any great 'food value', except for the carbohydrate it contains. Beers, on the other hand, *if naturally conditioned,* do contain a quantity of B vitamins from the yeast; obviously the lees need to be drunk as well in order to gain

TABLE 8

The Quantity of Metals & Vitamins Required per day, their approximate concentrations in drinks, and the volume of drink required to provide that amount.

Metal or Vitamin	Amount needed per day in mgms	Beer conc /100ml	Beer vol/day pints	Wine conc /100ml	Wine vol/day bottles
Calcium	1000	5-14	12-40	4-14	8-25
Iron	12	0.025	400	0.6	24
Carotene	5000 Units	Trace	~ ~	Trace	— ~
Thiamine	1.5	0.04	4300	0.03	700
Riboflavine	1.8	0.1	3.5	0.01	240
Nicotinic Ac	15	1	3	3	0.1
Ascorbic Acid	75	0	~	0	~

TABLE 9

Dietary needs per day and amount gained from Alcohol

	Daily Need in gm	Grams per 100 mls		
		Beer	Wine	Spirits
Carbohydrate	200	3-6	0.2-12.5	Trace
Fat	50	Trace	0	0
Protein	60	0.5	0.15	Trace
Calories	2000	30-70	60-160	220

this benefit. However, to repeat my earlier *caveat,* do not rely on alcoholic beverages for 'food'.

Herb wines that benefit the digestion will aid appetite, and hence general nutrition. So, the herbs discussed in the previous chapter are the ones most likely to aid nutrition. This is particularly true in the convalescent.

11 Sooth the Savage Breast

One of the most important points to remember about alcohol, as we have already seen, is that it is a depressant to the brain. Because of this action on the nerves, they do not respond so quickly to stimuli.

If you stick a pin in yourself, the pin stimulates (or activates) special nerves in the skin. These nerves send a message to the brain where it is decoded and a reply sent back along other nerves to the same spot to tell you that something is sticking into you, and that it hurts.

After a lot of alcohol, the nerves do not send accurate messages. And, rather like the slurred speech of the drunk, they get the message wrong so that the brain does not understand what is going on. As well as wrong information going to the brain, the brain, itself, is drunk and misunderstands the incorrect message. Result? Chaos!

With all this crossing of wires, the message received and translated by the skin is probably that something is pressing painlessly against you. If the nerves are very 'drunk', they will not respond to stimuli at all, so that the brain cannot warn you that something is wrong – i.e. you are anaesthetised.

Until about one hundred years ago, alcohol was used as *the* general anaesthetic agent. A bottle of rum, (for which, it is said, British sailors would go to Hell and back!), was given to a patient before operating. The stupor it induced enabled the surgeon to operate with a remarkably high success rate – not only in terms of surgical skill, but also of patient recovery! – and a considerable decrease in the amount of pain felt by the patient. (Happily, today, anaesthesia is a science not usually associated with hang overs!)

However, alcohol still plays a large part in the relief of pain. Rather than drinking the 'cure', it can be injected around the affected nerve. Some conditions are so painful that it is preferable to have an area of the body with no sensation at all rather than put up with the constant pain, or the taking of pain killing drugs that do not work. As many of the strong pain killers are addictive, it is worth trying to stop the pain by destroying the nerves. Pure alcohol is injected around the nerve causing the pain. The nerve is destroyed by the action of the alcohol denaturing the nerve. The same phenomenon that is seen when a haze develops in a wine that has been fortified.

Unfortunately, 'one' nerve is in fact a collection of perhaps many thousands of nerves (rather like the telephone cables beneath the pavement) so that it is impossible to select the one or two pieces of the nerve actually causing the pain. (Just as it is impossible, without opening the cable, to disconnect one particular phone wire). Hence the occasional apparent failure of these pain relieving injections.

Since, in order to stop the pain, the whole nerve may have to be destroyed, all the functions carried out by that nerve are arrested and an area of the body, larger than that affected by the pain becomes totally without sensation. However, if pain is sufficiently intractable, this is a small price to pay to be painfree. So, for all our advances in medicine, one of the oldest pain killers still has a rôle to play.

From one extreme of nerve deadening to the other, alcohol is a useful agent. In conditions of stress, a small tot of brandy or whisky will help steady the nerves. How much of this is due to the psychological effects of a drink is not certain, particularly as the effect can be almost instantaneous.

Wine is, however, better than spirits in this respect. Firstly, only a small amount of alcohol is required to reduce emotional stress. Secondly, presumably due to some of their congenerics, (higher alcohol which can cause hang overs and other metabolic problems), spirits can actually increase the degree of stress.

Do not, however, hope that tranquiliser pills will relax stress when accompanied by a drink. It is reasonable to state categorically that tranquilisers plus alcohol are a recipe for disaster.

Any drug that acts on the brain to depress it — and this includes tranquilisers, sedatives, anti-depressants, and sleeping pills — have the same effect on the brain as alcohol. However, *if you take any alcohol at all* while on almost any medical treatment, the resultant degree of drunkenness is far greater than would be expected from simply 'adding up' the effects of the tablets and the drink. The depressing effect of both on the brain and nerves is also potentiated, (or increased). Hence the warning on many pill bottles to avoid driving or operating machinery — a warning made imperative if foolish enough to add alcohol to the medicine.

This combination of alcohol and medicines has serious practical dangers. Many people simply do not heed warnings given to this effect. So, to repeat my warning, at the risk of boring you:

DO NOT, DESPITE ANY IMPRESSIONS TO THE CONTRARY, TAKE ALCOHOL IN ANY FORM MEDICINALLY WITHOUT CONSULTING YOUR OWN DOCTOR. WHILE ALCOHOL CAN, AND DOES, HAVE GOOD MEDICINAL PROPERTIES, IT IS VITAL TO REMEMBER THAT MOST MODERN MEDICINES REACT WITH ALCOHOL IN AN ADVERSE MANNER.

This is not merely to salve the collective medical conscience of the country. It is a real warning of possible fatal consequences if ignored.

Many people use sleeping pills — with their damaging side-effects. However, far better is a quiet bed-time drink. It does not need to be a large one. The sitting down, relaxing and unwinding whilst enjoying a drink will soon bring calm, refreshing sleep. A sleep which is nearer to normal than that induced by pills and encouraged by your own efforts in wine.

Earlier, we looked briefly at the effects of alcohol on behaviour. It is well worth looking at the effects of heavy drinking through the course of an evening's binge.

After the first drink at a party, the shy person will probably become talkative and extrovert due to relaxation of inhibitions. During this time, although the opposite may appear to be the truth, tests of ability are in fact decreasing in accuracy. This stage of the evening can be called 'Dizzy and Delightful', when the party is greatest fun and our drinker becomes the life and soul of the party.

Caught up in the excitement of the occasion, he continues to 'put them away' so that he becomes drunk — a condition obvious to all except our drinker. Attempts at the old test phrases like 'the

British Constitution' may produce results that vary from 'Brish Conshishoon' to utter gobbledegook! By now he has reached the stage of being 'Drunk'. Because of the loss of judgement that alcohol causes, glasses become broken as the mantelpiece moves a mysterious six inches away whenever he is putting things down!

Unfortunately, at this stage of drinking, judgement is so impaired that the reply to suggestions of temperance *(sic),* or 'easy going' are the tossing off of another couple.

By now, the party is beginning to deteriorate. Our erstwhile friend now alienates everybody by smashing the place up before sliding gracefully, if not crashing, to the floor, breaking yet more glasses in the process. If sufficiently idiotic to have drunk yet more before passing out, our friend may yet become our 'late friend' through inconsiderately dying on the sitting room floor from alcohol poisoning. Luckily, there is one saving grace. Alcohol in excess has the effect of stopping the stomach working. This may actually go on to cause vomiting — another effect of alcohol on the brain. This may disgust the onlooker, but it is quite probably a literal life saver, and may well explain why there are so few deaths from acute over-indulgence.

This may sound amusing; it is in fact very serious. Every year sees reports in the national press detailing details from such idiotic behaviour.

Yet again, the message is clear. Enjoy a drink or two. But, do not drink to excess. Short term results can be just as fatal as long term effects of excess.

Herbs

Most of the herbs that have some claim to help the nervous system are those that have some tranquilising action. There are few that can claim to 'cure' diseases of the brain, though some are said to help in depression.

When we come to examine the herbs that possibly help the nervous system, there is one enormous difficulty. Many of them are extremely dangerous. Those that are safe are discussed later. Some of the plants to avoid are:

Aconite	Betony
Asafoetida	Bryony, White

Chestnut, Sweet
Cramp bark
Feverfew
Galanga
Gelsemium
Horehound, Black
Iceland moss
Kola
Lady's Slipper

Lettuce, Wild
Mistletoe
Motherwort
Passionflower
St Johns Wort
Scullcap
Squaw vine
Valerian

As before, with herbs or plants that have been discussed earlier in the book, you are directed to the appropriate Chapter and page.

Betony

According to herbalists, this herb increases the circulation in the head. It is also a relaxant, and has some action in stimulating the digestion. Other uses include the treatment of sinusitis. It has never appeared in the pharmacopoeia.

★ Betony Wine

Ingredient	Quantity per gallon	Quantity per 5 litres
Betony	½ lb	250 gms
White grape concentrate	1 pint	500 mls
Sugar	to SG 70	to SG 70
Vitamin B_1	6 mg	6 mg
Water	to volume	to volume

For the recommended additives, see Page 53.

Wash and chop the betony. Boil for ten minutes. Allow to cool and add the other ingredients, nutrients and an active yeast starter. Ferment for four days on the pulp, stirring daily. Strain, make to volume, and ferment to dryness under air lock. Rack and mature in the usual way. Sweeten to taste as described in Chapter 5.

Chamomile

See Chapter 9; page 93.

Chamomile Wine

See Chapter 9; page 93.

Coltsfoot

See Chapter 12; page 125.

Coltsfoot Wine

See Chapter 12; page 125.

Cowslip

The dried flowers are used as a tranquiliser — both for 'nerves' and as a sleeping draught. This sedative action has benefits for persistent coughs such as are seen in chronic bronchitis and whooping cough. Although not listed in the old pharmacopoeia, many recent editions (from many lands), give the root of the plant a place as an expectorant.

✳ Cowslip Wine

Ingredient	Quantity per gallon	Quantity per 5 litres
Cowslip flowers	2 lbs	1 kg
Raisins	1 lb	500 gms
Sugar	to SG 70	to SG 70
Yeast		
Vitamin B_1	6 mg	6 mg
Water	to volume	to volume

For the recommended additives, see Page 53.

Wash and chop the raisins. Rinse the flowers in a colander. Mix both in 4 pints water and boil for twenty minutes. Strain and add the sugar. When cool, add the nutrients and an active yeast starter. When fermentation dies down, make to volume, and ferment under airlock to dryness. Rack and mature in the usual way. Sweeten to taste as described in Chapter 5.

Hops

See Chapter 9; page 96.

Hop Wine

See Chapter 9; page 96.

Lemon Balm

See Chapter 9; page 97.

Lemon Balm Wine

See Chapter 9; page 97.

Passion Flower

Used in nervous complaints as a tranquiliser and sleeping draught. It is also used in some stomach conditions — basically, again, as a sedative or soothing preparation. The pharmacopeia is dubious about some of these properties, particularly about its use as a pain reliever in neuralgia.

✷ Passionfruit Wine

Ingredient	Quantity per gallon	Quantity per 5 litres
Passionfruit juice	24 oz	700 mls
Sugar	to SG 70	to SG 70
Yeast	Tokay	
Vitamin B_1	6 mg	6 mg
Water	to volume	to volume

For the recommended additives, see Page 53.

First, make the sugar into a syrup, and then mix all the other ingredients. Add the nutrients and an active yeast starter. When fermentation dies down, make to volume. Ferment under airlock to dryness. Rack and mature in the usual way. This wine benefits from keeping for at least six months. Sweeten to taste as described in Chapter 5.

Peach

Although not listed in all herbals, peach leaves are considered to have sedative and anti sickness properties. The latter, not medically recommended, leads to the suggestion of using them for sickness of pregnancy. However, as they are also laxative, this does not seem a good idea. Another use is the relief of chronic bronchitis. A magical cure for warts is to rub the wart with peach leaves. The leaves are then buried, and by the time they have decayed, the wart will have disappeared. Apart from the oil, similar to *Apricot Oil,* there is no mention of peaches in the pharmacopoeiae.

Peach Wine

See Chapter 3; page 21.

Rosemary

Used for many problems of the nerves. From migraine to tension, from palpitations to depression. It is also used as a treatment for flatulence and in some liver problems. The oil is used on the scalp to prevent premature balding and dandruff. Rosemary wine is considered a specific for palpitations. Mixed with *Coltsfoot,* their dried leaves smoked as a herbal tobacco is supposed to be a harmless but most effective treatment for asthma. This last use must be viewed with grave disquiet. The tars present in 'real' cigarettes may be the major toxic chemicals, but the smoke itself, and carbon monoxide are especially poisonous and harmful. It is now generally agreed that smoking any compound is harmful. The old pharmacopoeiae list oil of rosemary as a compound which, apart from its use as a hair lotion and a linament, is useful as an insect repellant. Recent editions mention the fragrant property of the oil, and also the 'former use' in gynaecological problems and for inducing sweating.

✱ **Rosemary Wine**

Ingredient	Quantity per gallon	Quantity per 5 litres
Rosemary	2 pints	1 litre
Raisins	1 lb	500 gms
Sugar	to SG 70	to SG 70
Tannin	½ teaspoon	2.5 gms
Citric acid	1 teaspoon	5 gms
Yeast		
Vitamin B$_1$	6 mg	6 mg
Water	to volume	to volume

For the recommended additives, see Page 53.

Wash the rosemary and bring to the boil in 6 pints (3 litres) water. Add the raisins (washed and chopped). Sulphite, cover, and leave for twenty four hours. Add the rest of the ingredients, nutrients and an active yeast starter. Ferment on the pulp for one week. Strain, make to volume, and finish fermenting to dryness under air lock. Rack and mature as usual. Sweeten to taste as described in Chapter 5.

12 A Breath of Fresh Air

When we come to look at the effect of alcohol on breathing, there is little to add to what has already been said about alcohol and its actions on the brain. Because breathing is controlled by the brain, alcohol will, in common with depressing other brain activities, depress respiration.

Alcohol is excreted partly through the lungs — a fact made use of in the Breathalyser. The amount of alcohol present in the air breathed out being in direct relation with the amount of alcohol in the body.

There is, however, one important aspect of winemaking and brewing that does affect breathing. That is *metabisulphite* — either the sodium or potassium salts. Or, in its commonest form, Campden Tablets. It is also known by such names as sulphate, sodium met., or sulphite.

The active ingredient of sodium metabisulphite is *sulphur dioxide* — the commonest sterilising agent used in winemaking and brewing. To start by allaying one of the foremost fears of today — it is not a cancer causing agent.

When metabisulphite is dissolved in water it enters solution and undergoes the following chemical reaction:

$$Na_2S_2O_5 \;+\; \;+\; H_2O \;\rightarrow\; 2NaHSO_3$$
Sodium Metabisulphite + Water → Sodium Bisulphite

This bisulphite then changes into sulphur dioxide and an alkali, *Sodium hydroxide.*

$$2Na\,HSO_3 \;\rightarrow\; SO_2 \;+\; NaOH$$
Sodium Bisulphite → Sulphur Dioxide + Sodium Hydroxide

When in aqueous solution (i.e. in water), the sulphur dioxide combines with the water to form firstly *sulphurous acid* and then *sulphuric acid.*

$$SO_2 + H_2O \rightarrow H_2SO_3 + O_2 \rightarrow H_2SO_4$$

Sulphur Dioxide + Water → Sulphurous Acid + Oxygen → Sulphuric Acid

Both sulphur dioxide and sulphuric acid are gases which will escape from solution to enter the surrounding atmosphere. If present in very much more than trace concentrations, it can be detected by the average person who will notice the characteristically marked pungent smell. A sensitive nose will be able to smell sulphur dioxide at a level of two or three parts per million.

In America, legislation has been passed which limits the maximum permissable atmospheric level to 5 ppm in enclosed spaces. If the concentration is liable to be greater than this, special extractor fans and protective clothing are legal requirements.

We have seen the result of dissolving sulphite in water. Sulphur dioxide, as well as small quantities of sulphurous and sulphuric acids, are produced. These are released into the atmosphere and will be recognised by all winemakers and brewers, in incautious moments, to be extremely irritating.

It is, therefore, imperative for everybody when using metabisulphite in any form, but especially when concentrated as a sterilising solution for cleaning equipment, to take extreme caution not to inhale the fumes.

When using a strong solution it is a sensible precaution to use it only in open spaces, or to make sure that the room is well ventilated with either an open window or extractor fan.

Under no circumstances check to see if the sulphite solution is still potent by sniffing at it because, if it is still concentrated, the results of a lungful of what is effectively sulphuric acid (to put it in extreme terms), will be neither grateful nor comforting.

Research done in America has shown that low concentrations of sulphur dioxide (0.5-5 ppm) for as little as five minutes produced significant changes in lung function for up to one hour after breathing the gas. Most subjects who were exposed to as little as 3 ppm for only three minutes had symptoms of irritation of the throat; some were even affected enough to make them cough. One of the problems of breathing sulphur dioxide is that it causes

120 constriction of the breathing passages so that the body's ability to

rid itself of the gas is actually slowed down and reduced. (Exercise can speed up excretion of sulphur dioxide.)

In another study, more than 10% of asthmatic patients had their symptoms made worse after drinking fruit squash. All the drinks tested contained sulphur dioxide, or sodium benzoate, or tartrazine as a preservative. Of the patients tested, half reacted adversely to sulphur dioxide; most of these people were both young and asthma sufferers. It may therefore be that some of the allergies to wine encountered may not be due to the wines themselves but sulphur dioxide.

Since the Clean Air Act came into force the thick yellow London smog is now, thankfully, a thing of the past. There must be many who can still remember, with loathing, the thick taste of fog in the throat; a fog which actually burned. All due to Sulphur Dioxide.

It can only be considered folly for a sufferer from chest disease to worsen his condition by inhaling high concentrations of further irritants. In the same way in which the smoker is advised to desist from his habit, so too should the winemaker from the inhalation of any other substance — in this case sulphur dioxide.

It is often convenient to blame a substance such as sulphur dioxide for one's chest condition, but it is most unlikely that anyone has made wine long enough in this country, inhaling sufficient sulphur dioxide, (unless a saturated solution) to cause permanent lung damage. Instead, it is much more likely that with the passage of time other irritants such as tobacco, industrial fumes, vehicular fumes, and all the waste of a civilised nation have conspired together to cause the lung problem. Inhaling sulphur dioxide fumes when winemaking merely exacerbates the condition.

What then can be done to minimise any problem from one of the most useful of winemaking's adjuncts? Firstly, it cannot be emphasised strongly enough that, if you do suffer from bronchitis or asthma, you must take great care when winemaking or brewing not to inhale sulphur dioxide fumes.

As we have said earlier, the use of sulphur dioxide must be in low concentrations and the sterilising of equipment must be performed with non-irritant substances — or better still, by some one else! Apart from safety, one of the most boring and back breaking jobs in winemaking and brewing is avoided! If you must use the substance yourself, the least you can do is to use an industrial mask which absorbs some, although not all, of the fumes.

Make sure that the *Vent Axia* fan is switched on in the kitchen when sulphiting your wines or rinsing equipment.

Do not stick your nose into the equipment or the sulphite jar.

For those who do wish to use sulphite, the simple routine is as follows: When preparing most wine musts it is a good idea to sulphite the mixture of base ingredients to ensure sterility. Not only does it aid extraction of colour and flavour, but it also makes sure that any fermentation inhibitor, like chlorine, has a chance to disperse before pitching the yeast.

Once fermentation has finished, sulphite the wine. This aids clearing, prevents oxidation, and helps prolong the 'shelf life' of the wine.

Whatever any one may feel about sulphite, there is no need to worry when using it as a sterilising agent for equipment. After thoroughly cleaning the equipment, a rinse with strong sulphite solution (remembering the cautions) will ensure that it is sterile. Before use, rinse with clean water from the tap; this is effectively guaranteed sterile. Thus, the equipment is clean and sterile, but no danger lurks for anyone who may be sensitive to sulphite.

Herbs

Most herbal remedies that have uses in chest conditions are for some degree of cough — from a 'tickly throat' to chronic bronchitis. Those plants with sedative properties often find a place in the treatment of digestive problems, while some are used as tranquilisers.

Angelica

See Chapter 9; page 88.

Angelica Wine

See Chapter 9; page 88.

Aniseed

See Chapter 9; page 89.

Apricot

Apricots have a food value in their fresh state — they contain several vitamins. A gum exuded by the tree is similar to acacia gum, and can be used as the basis for a gargle. The pharmacopoeia lists a preparation made from the seeds used in cough medicines. There is an oil, also listed, from the kernel. It has nutrient value, and is the base for some cosmetics.

Apricot Wine

See Chapter 3; page 22.

Blackberry

The leaves are possibly still used as a folk remedy for burns and scalds — hence one of its alternative names *Scaldhead*. From early times, both fruit and flower were used as a specific against snake bite. A hair dye made from the leaves is said to colour hair black. Medicinally, the leaves are used in the treatment of diarrhoea, as well as for the relief of coughs and colds. The pharmacopoeia still lists the first of these uses.

* Blackberry Wine

Ingredient	Quantity per gallon	Quantity per 5 litres
Blackberries	4 lbs	2 kg
Sugar	to SG 70	to SG 70
Yeast		
Vitamin B_1	6 mg	6 mg
Water	to volume	to volume

For the recommended additives, see Page 53.

Prepare a yeast starter. When almost ready, collect the blackberries. Wash and crush them, and mix them with all the ingredients in six pints of water. Add the starter and ferment on the pulp for three days. Rack, make to volume, and ferment to dryness under air lock. Rack and mature in the usual way. Sweeten to taste as described in Chapter 5. This wine will need at least six months maturation.

Caraway

The seeds which are well known in the kitchen, are also used herbally in the treatment of indigestion and colic, as well as in the relief of chronic bronchitis. These uses are given in the old pharmacopoeia; in later editions, its use is limited to the treatment of infant colic *(caraway water)*, and as a flavouring for children's medicines.

*   Caraway Wine

Ingredient	Quantity per gallon	Quantity per 5 litres
Caraway seeds	1 oz	30 gms
Raisins	1 lb	450 gms
Lemons	3	3
Sugar	to SG 70	to SG 70
Weak tea	2 pints	1 litre
Yeast		
Vitamin B$_1$	6 mg	6 mg
Water	to volume	to volume

For the recommended additives, see Page 53.

Add the seeds to 6 pints (3 litres) water. Bring to the boil to extract the flavour. Pour over the washed and chopped raisins, add the sugar. Mix thoroughly. When cool, add the nutrients, tea, lemon juice and an active yeast starter. Ferment on the pulp for one week. Rack, make to volume, and ferment to dryness under air lock. Rack and mature in the usual way. Sweeten to taste as described in Chapter 5.

Chamomile

See Chapter 9; page 93.

Chamomile Wine

See Chapter 9; page 93.

Coltsfoot

Its botanical name *Tussilago* gives its herbal action — a cough remedy. Used herbally for coughs and asthma, both the flowers and the leaves have a place in the pharmacopoeia for this action.

★   ## Coltsfoot Wine

Ingredient	Quantity per gallon	Quantity per 5 litres
Coltsfoot flowers	1 gallon	4 litres

For the recommended additives, see Page 53.

Other ingredients and method as for *Hawthorn Flower Wine* — Chapter 7; page 66.

Comfrey

See Chapter 8; page 77.

Comfrey Wine

See Chapter 8; page 78.

Cowslip

See Chapter 11; page 115.

Cowslip Wine

See Chapter 11; page 115.

Elder Flower

See Chapter 8; page 75.

Elderflower Wine

See Chapter 3; page 25.

Elecampane

Used particularly for bronchitis to aid the production of phlegm, it had wide use when tuberculosis was rife. It is also soothing to the digestion.

★ Elecampane Wine

Ingredient	Quantity per gallon	Quantity per 5 litres
Elecampane root	1 lb	500 gms
Sugar	to SG 70	to SG 70
White grape concentrate	1 pint	500 mls
Yeast		
Vitamin B_1	6 mg	6 mg
Water	to volume	to volume

For the recommended additives, see Page 53.

Pour 6 pints (3 litres) of *boiling* water over the roots. After fifteen minutes, strain off. Add the sugar and grape concentrate, mix well. When cool, add the nutrients and an active yeast starter. When fermentation dies down, make to volume, and ferment under air lock to dryness. Rack, mature and sweeten as usual.

Ginger

See Chapter 7; page 65.

Ginger Wine

See Chapter 7; page 66.

Golden Rod

See Chapter 8; page 78.

Golden Rod Wine

See Chapter 8; page 79.

Heartsease

To my mind a far more attractive name than the more prosaic *Pansy*. It is used herbally as a treatment for removal of excess fluid, to aid a non productive cough, and as a laxative. It does not appear to have ever been included in the pharmacopoeia .

∗ Sparkling Heartsease Wine

Ingredient	Quantity per gallon	Quantity per 5 litres
White Pansy flowers	½ lb	250 gms
Sugar	to SG 70	to SG 70
Lemons	3	3
Oranges	3	3
Barley	1 lb	500 gms
Yeast		
Vitamin B_1	6 mg	6 mg
Water	to volume	to volume

For the recommended additives, see Page 53.

Skin the oranges and lemons, being careful to remove all the pith. Slice the citrus fruit. Place in 5 pints (2.5 litres) water with the flowers and barley, and bring to the boil. Simmer for ten minutes. Strain the liquid over the sugar. Allow to cool and add the nutrients and an active yeast starter. When the fermentation dies down, make to volume then continue fermentation under air lock to SG 10. Rack carefully into champagne bottles. Do not use damaged bottles, and above all make sure that the bottles are designed to withstand the pressure that will be generated during the rest of fermentation. If you wish to sweeten, do so now (as described in Chapter 5). Use proper champagne closures and mature for three months in a cold place to minimise the chances of exploding bottles. Chill before opening.

If you prefer, the wine can be fermented to dryness as in the 'normal' method outlined in the book.

Liquorice

As well as its use in cough medicines and as an anti-inflammatory, liquorice is used as an agent for reducing gastric acidity (in other words, for the relief of indigestion). It is said to have an action in reducing the effects of steroid overdose. Apart from the latter all these uses are listed in the old pharmacopoeia — which is included in later editions as a treatment for Addisons disease and rheumatoid arthritis. However, since the root can cause fluid retention, it seems unwise to use it in cases of heart failure or, indeed, Addison's disease.

✳ Liquorice Wine

Ingredient	Quantity per gallon	Quantity per 5 litres
Liquorice root	2 oz	60 gms
White grape concentrate	1 pint	500 mls
Sugar	to SG 70	to SG 70
Yeast		
Vitamin B_1	6 mg	6 mg
Water	to volume	to volume

For the recommended additives, see Page 53.

Mix all the ingredients, including the sliced root. Ferment on the pulp for three days. Rack, make to volume, and ferment to dryness under air lock. Rack and mature in the usual way. Sweeten to taste as described in Chapter 5.

Lovage

See Chapter 9; page 97.

Lovage Wine

See Chapter 9; page 98.

Rose Hip

As well as being one of the best natural sources of Vitamin C, the syrup from the hips is a good cough soother. It also has some action on the inflamed intestine in diarrhoea. In the old pharmacopoeia the hip is listed as the base for linctuses, as a flavouring agent, and in the making of *electuaries* (medicines based on honey). Recently, the pharmacopoeia only allows the rose hip as a source of ascorbic acid. (They contain more than blackcurrants).

✳ Rose Hip Wine

Ingredient	Quantity per gallon	Quantity per 5 litres
Rose Hips	2 lbs	1 kg
Citric acid	1 teaspoon	5 gms
Sugar	to SG 70	to SG 70
Yeast		
Vitamin B$_1$	6 mg	6 mg
Water	to volume	to volume

For the recommended additives, see Page 53.

Wash the hips thoroughly, then either halve or crush them. Pour 5 pints boiling water over them, add the sugar and mix well. When cool, add the nutrients and an active yeast starter. Ferment on the pulp for ten days. Stir daily. Strain off, make to volume, and finish fermentation under air lock. Rack and mature in the usual way. Sweeten to taste as described in Chapter 5.

If you cannot find fresh hips, either use ½ lb (250 gms) of dried hips or use Rosehip syrup which is obtainable from your chemist.

Rue

Rue is used herbally as a treatment for bronchitis and croup. It must not be used during pregnancy. It is also an emetic (it will make you sick), so large doses are taboo. It can also be used as a tranquiliser in hysteria. The fresh leaves were used, bruised, to ease the pain of sciatica. Most of these properties are listed in the old pharmacopoeia; more recently, its antispasmodic action is noted, together with its violent side effects.

*   Rue Wine

Ingredient	Quantity per gallon	Quantity per 5 litres
Rue	1 lb	500 gms
Raisins	1 lb	500 gms
Sugar	to SG 70	to SG 70
Yeast		
Vitamin B$_1$	6 mg	6 mg
Water	to volume	to volume

For the recommended additives, see Page 53.

Wash and chop the rue and raisins. Boil together in 4 pints (2 litres) water for twenty minutes. Strain. Add the sugar and mix well. When cool, add the nutrients and an active yeast starter. When fermentation dies down, make to volume and ferment under air lock to dryness. Rack and mature as usual. Sweeten to taste as described in Chapter 5.

As this herb can cause vomiting in large quantities, it is not recommended that large quantities of this wine be drunk at one time.

Thyme

See Chapter 9; page 101.

Thyme Wine

See Chapter 9; page 102.

Among the herbs and plants mentioned in herbals that are not recommended for winemaking are the following. As always, if in doubt about the safety of any plant, do not use it.

Bryony, White	Horehound, White	Mouse-ear
Chestnut, Sweet	Horseradish	Mullein
Cudweed, Marsh	Horsetail	Plantain
Echinacea	Ipecacuanha	Pleurisy Root
Ephedra	Irish Moss	Ribwort
Euphorbia	Jimson Weed	Squill
Garlic	Linseed	Sundew
Germander, Wall	Lobelia	Valerian
Grindelia	Lungwort	Wild Cherry Bark
Henbane	Marshmallow	

13 Diabetes

Diabetes, or *Sugar Diabetes* as it is known to many people, is by no means an uncommon disease. Surveys have shown that, as with so many other diseases, 'civilisation' brings in its wake an increase in the occurence of this condition.

Some researchers have suggested that it may be present in as many as 7% in some populations. One of the most likely explanations for this high figure is that, with increasing standards of living, come an increase in the intake of dietary carbohydrate, (sugar, sweets, cream, and cakes). Since the body can only utilize a certain amount of this form of food, the excess has to be excreted. This is done by the kidneys letting the sugar out of the body in the urine – hence the layman's term 'sugar diabetes'.

There are two main types of diabetes. The first is known as the *Juvenile* type because it is usually diagnosed first in children. The other form is known as the *Elderly* type because it usually becomes apparent in later years. In fact, both types cause the same problems to the sufferer and the terms are simply used as an easy way of classifying the disease.

Diabetes is a disease of the metabolism (the utilisation of foodstuffs by the body). It is due to the inability of the *pancreas* (or sweetbreads) to produce enough of a hormone called *Insulin* which removes any sugar not immediately required by the body from the blood stream and stores it in the liver and muscles.

Since in diabetes the excess sugar is not removed from the blood, the blood sugar level rises; and it is this excess sugar which causes the disease.

In the juvenile form of the disease, the pancreas does not contain the cells which make the hormone. The elderly type is largely self-induced. We have already seen how, with increasing age and promotion, there is an increase in eating habits. Since higher ranking jobs tend to be more sedentary than their lower grades, weight is more easily gained. Obesity predisposes to diabetes and, since 80% of diabetics are first seen when in the second half of life and are mostly obese, it follows that a disciplined régime both of diet and exercise will do a great deal to prevent this condition.

If diabetes is not controlled — by diet, tablets, or insulin — it can be a dangerous disease. Because of the increase in both food and alcohol consumption in this country, it is well worth considering this problem in relation to type.

Sugar in the form of glucose is the chief fuel of the body. It is normally stored as glycogen — a chemical which is simply long chains of glucose — in the liver and muscle. Diabetics cannot store sugar; nor can they utilise it. So, although there may be plenty of fuel, they have to make use of the reserve food of the body — fat. Unfortunately, fat provides not only food but also poisons the body when it is broken down in large amounts. Thus, a diabetic without treatment will literally die of self-poisoning from the toxic waste produced in fat metabolism — after going into a diabetic coma.

To prevent this, treatment is vitally important. As well as insulin injections, or tablets, the diet must be carefully controlled (and, therefore, the weight). It is no use working out the treatment required for a diet of 100 gms of carbohydrate a day and the patient then consuming 150 gms. The result may be as though the patient was having no treatment.

Because diabetes affects all parts of the metabolism (and not just carbohydrate as is often thought) the daily diet may be specified for all food stuffs. While carbohydrate is carefully specified, other foods are controlled largely by the patient's weight.

Tablets given to diabetics have the effect of stimulating the pancreas to produce insulin and so stop the blood sugar rising to dangerous levels. This is usually the treatment for the elderly type of diabetic. Some diabetics — usually the juvenile type — cannot make insulin because their pancreas does not contain the cells responsible for its production. These people require insulin.

Insulin is a hormone which helps sugar enter cells in the liver and muscle where the glucose is polymerized into glycogen. Insulin also acts as a catalyst in one of the chemical reactions which take place to make the glycogen.

To understand the effects of alcohol on a diabetic we must look again at the breakdown of alcohol and sugar in the body. Both are broken down finally in the same way. This means that even if one drinks a completely dry wine, one molecule of alcohol is equivalent to a quarter of a molecule of sugar in terms of energy provided for the body. Alternatively, one molecule of sugar is the same as four molecules of alcohol.

Or, that one gram molecule of sugar equals four gram molecules of alcohol. One gram molecule is the weight of a substance equal to the sum of its constituent atomic weights in grams: i.e. 180 grams of sugar = 184 grams of alcohol.

Logically, this is what one would expect. However, and here's the rub, one gram of sugar provides 3.75 calories of energy, while one gram of alcohol provides seven calories. This is because some of the food carbohydrate cannot be utilised since some is present in the form of cellulose – a substance we cannot digest. On the other hand, all the alcohol ingested can be absorbed and utilised. Hence the difference in calorific values. This means in day to day dieting terms that a 100 ml glass of dry wine with an alcohol content of 10% will contain seventy calories.

However, before a diabetic begins to drink, he must take into account not only the alcohol, but also the sugar, content.

If a sweet wine has a final specific gravity of 102 – the minimum for a sweet wine – it will contain six grams of free sugar per 100 mls. Unlike 'normal' food, this carbohydrate is all available (i.e. it is all utilised by the body) and so will also have a calorific value of about seven calories per gram.

Thus, this wine will contain 70 calories from the alcohol and a further 42 from the residual sugar – a total of 112 calories. This represents, in many cases, ten percent of the total calories permitted in the daily diet. Once you have allowed for the loss of vitamins, proteins and polyunsaturated fats essential to health, it does not leave a great deal of room for 'fillers' like bread and potatoes – let alone 'sweets'.

The following table lists some commercial drinks and the calories and carbohydrates contained in 100 ml of each.

TABLE 10

**Carbohydrate and Calorific Content of some
Commercial Drinks**

	Carbohydrate gm/100 ml	Calories per 100 ml
Vermouths and Aromatised Wines		
Dry French Vermouth	3.3	133
Martini Extra Dry	3.6	134
Cinzano Rosso	12.4	170
Dubonnet	15	180
Martini Rosso	16.2	185
Sparkling Wines		
Veuve du Vernay Brut	1	62
Demi-sec German	4	64
Veuve Du Vernay Demi-Sec	4	74
Medium Dry Champagne	1.5	81
Dry Table Wines		
French or Italian Dry	0.58	79
Muscadet	0.12	85
Tavel Rosé	0.3	85
Single vineyard Bordeaux Red	0.39	86
Sancerre	0.52	90
Chablis	0.13	92
Medium Table Wines		
Hock	2.5	73
Anjou Rosé	5.4	85
Vouvray Demi-Sec	3.1	89
Medium Dry French or Italian	2.3	93
Medium Sweet French or Italian	2.3	93
Fortified Wines		
Harvey's Fino Sherry	.2	97
Harvey's Dry Sherry	.2	100
Domecq La Ina Fino Sherry	.99	108
Harvey's Bristol Dry Sherry	3.5	115
Cockburn's Ruby Port	8.5	150
Harvey's Bristol Cream	12.5	175
Spirits 70% Proof	0	222

The above values are approximate and will vary with different
shipments and vintages.

From this table, you can see that a tot of whisky is just over ten percent of the daily calorific allowance in a 1,000 calorie diet; while a pint of strong ale is over one-third. This is a valid point for not only the diabetic, but also everyone who is overweight. A night on the beer can easily mean that you should starve yourself for a weekend in order to prevent increasing obesity.

It is not difficult to see why so many experts have barred alcohol from diabetic diets. However, we shall see how, by lowering the alcohol content and *ensuring no residual sugar,* the diabetic can enjoy the occasional glass of wine. *Provided, that is, he or she first obtains the sanction of their doctor. Diabetics having treatment by tablets must especially follow this injunction. Alcohol can actually cause a marked rise in blood sugar with some of the diabetic tablets. The group of tablets known as the* Sulphylonureas *include such tablets as* **Diabinase, Glucophage,** *and* **Rastinon.**

The other condition of drinking alcohol must be to adjust the diet accordingly.

It is important to stress that excess alcohol is bad — particularly on a calorifically controlled diet because of the lack of vitamins in alcohol. So, again, there is the need to stress the need for caution and moderation for all diabetics.

So, having said what is not allowed, let us see if we can arrive at a compromise.

The first thing to do is to list the essential conditions for any alcoholic drink for the diabetic. These are:

(a) Fermentation must be complete.
(b) There must be no residual fermentable base as tested for by specific gravity and sugar testing kits.
(c) The calorific value of the drink must not be so high as to impair a sensible balance in the daily dietary intake.
(d) Any sweetening must be done by using low calorie artificial sweetening agents.
(e) Forbidden foodstuffs should be avoided in the recipes.
(f) Small amounts only should be consumed.
(g) The original gravity must be lower than in 'normal' recipes.

Since one of the prime considerations for diabetics is strict calorie control, it is vital to know the ingredients and their calorific contents precisely.

When dining out one is limited in this knowledge. Apart from diabetic beers and soft drinks, only Germany has wine laws which include a class for diabetic wines. By this law, a special label denotes a diabetic wine and its contents. The alcohol content must be measured exactly so that you can calculate the calorific value of your wine.

As sugars are absorbed almost directly, their presence is undesirable as the blood sugar will be increased rapidly. To avoid this, check for residual sugar with the tests listed in Table 11 after fermentation has finished. Details of these tests are given in Chapter 4.

TABLE 11

Essential Tests to be done on Diabetic Wines

---

(1) SG of natural sugar adjusted to final volume.
(2) SG of added sugar.
(3) Total Original gravity.
(4) Final Gravity.
(5) Make temperature corrections for SG readings.
(6) Alcohol content.
(7) Residual sugar.
(8) Calorific value of drinking volume.
(9) Test for starch. This is not fermentable, but it can be
      utilised by the body.
(10) Acidity.

In a wine, a specific gravity reading of 0 or below should mean no surplus carbohydrate. However, in beers, dextrins which are broken down in the body to sugar, do not react with sugar testing reagents.

Sweetening after the final fermentation has stabilised is best done with one of the artificial sweeteners. I have used *Sweetex* liquid with good results. But, beware of overdoing it. I ruined two gallons of Brown Ale by adding six drops!

Work out the calorific value of the drink as described, and exchange a portion of your daily carbohydrate allowance for the drink.

Should fining be required, there are no worries about adding to the calorific value of the wine since gelatin or egg white (two commonly used, edible agents) are low in carbohydrate. Bentonite, a non-edible substance, carries no risk in this direction.

Although diabetics have to be beware of their choice of foodstuffs, there is not much risk when the 'forbidden fruits' are made into wine. This is because a fruit with a high natural sugar content requires less additional sugar to make the must up to the original gravity. Nonetheless, a list of fruits and vegetables used in winemaking that have a high calorific value is useful if only as a warning to beware of excess sugar additions. (See Table 14.)

It is best, again in the interests of calorie control, to keep the alcohol content below 10%. This means an Original Gravity of not more than 70. In other words, the Specific Gravity should be less than 1070.

TABLE 12

Maximum Permitted Sugar Additions per gallon of Diabetic Wine. Calculated from the SG of the juice made up to 1 gallon or 5 litres.

SG of Juice	Maximum Sugar	
	oz/Gallon	gms/5 Litres
70+	Dilute	
70	0	0
65	2.75	17
60	4.75	30
55	7	44
50	9	57
45	11	70
40	13.25	83
35	15.5	97
30	17.5	110
25	19.5	123
20	21.5	136
15	23.75	149
10	25.75	163
5	28	176

So, prepare the fruit in the normal way. Take the specific gravity of the juice or pulp, and its volume. From this, work out the gravity the ingredients will have in the final volume. If your fruit accounts for more than 20 units of gravity you can add no more than 50 units of specific gravity of sugar per gallon. In other words, no more than $21\frac{1}{2}$ oz per gallon of sugar. (See Table 12).

Do not add all this sugar in one go. Instead, to be absolutely sure of complete fermentation, practice exponential feeding. To do this, add 2 oz of sugar per gallon every time the gravity falls to 1.005. If you do not have the equipment to measure the gravity, make the sugar additions every four or five days until the sugar permitted has been added.

To ensure proper fermentation, correct acid balance is important. If you are using a mixture of acids, at least one quarter of the acid used should be citric acid because this acid stimulates a healthy fermentation. For the same reason nutrients are important. (See Chapter 6 on Additives.)

TABLE 13

The Expected Final Gravity (F.G.) from Different Original Gravities (O.G.)

O.G.	F.G.	Degrees drop	Potential alcohol content	sugar oz./gal.	gm./litre
1070	.992	78	11.2	30	189
1065	.993	72	10.4	28	176
1060	.994	66	9.6	25	163
1055	.995	60	8.8	23	149
1050	.995	55	8.3	21	136
1045	.997	48	7.0	19	123
1040	.997	43	6.5	17	110
1035	.998	37	5.8	15	97
1030	1.000	30	4.9	13	83
1025	1.001	24	4.1	11	70
1020	1.002	18	3.3	9	57

Before racking the wine, make sure that fermentation has been complete. Reference to Table 13 shows the expected final gravity from a given original gravity. Again, if you do not have a hydrometer to measure this, wait a few days after you think fermentation has finished before racking.

Once the wine has finished fermenting, rack and mature in the normal way. If needed, use finings as discussed in Chapter 4.

Sweetening is best carried out to taste. To do this use liquid artificial sweeteners. See Chapter 5 for a full description of the technique.

It is important to remember that wines which are low in alcohol do not keep so long and are more liable to infection than stronger wines. Hence, it is wisest to sulphite them at a rate of 50-100 ppm (1-2 campden tablets per gallon). Take care with this, because sulphite can be bad for a diabetic. If you decide not to sulphite a wine, take great care with sterilising equipment and bottles since infection can easily gain access. And, as importantly, the wine will not have a very long shelf life.

When we come to look for herbs that are said to have a beneficial action on diabetes, there are a limited number only. Just how effective they are, is not possible to say. But, I would emphasise that they can in no way be assumed to act in parallel with your diabetic drugs. Any treatment you may be on must be continued with. The recipes given, and the pharmacological notes, are merely curios that may have had some effect in days gone; today, they canot be used in any medical way.

TABLE 14

Carbohydrate and Calorific Content of Common Winemaking Ingredients

Ingredient	Calories/ 100 gm	Amount of ingredient containing 100 carbohydrate	Amount used/ gallon of wine
Apple Cooker, Dessert	35, 50	120 gm	Variable
Apricot Fresh, Dried	28, 183	180 gm, 30 gm	2 lb
Banana without skin	77	60 gm	2 lb
Blackberry	30	160 gm	3½ lb
Cherry	46	120 gm	6 lb
Currant	21–29	180 gm	3 lb
Damson	34	150 gm	4 lb
Dates whole stoned	214, 248	20 gm, 15 gm	1 lb
Fig Green, Dried	41, 214	120 gm, 20 gm	2 lb
G'berry Unripe, Ripe	17, 37	300 gm, 120 gm	4 lb
Grapes	60	60 gm	15 lb
Greengage – stoned	45	90 gm	4 lb
Oranges Jaffa	35	4 fruit, 130 gm	6 fruit
Peach Fresh, Dried	37, 213	120 gm, 20 gm	3 lb, 1 lb
Pear	30–40	120 gm	4 lb
P'apple Fresh, Tinned	40, 70	90 gm	4 fruit, 1 lb 3 oz
Plum	20–30	120 gm	4 lb
Prunes	161	30 gm	6 lb
Raisins	247	15 gm	3 lb
Raspberry	25	180 gm	2 lb
Rhubarb	6	800 gm	3 lb
Strawberry	26	180 gm	4 lb
Sultanas	249	15 gm	3 lb
Grapefruit juice	24	180 gm	1 pint
Lemon juice	1.6	625 ml	½ pint
Orange Unsweetened	38	100 ml	1 pint
Pineapple Unsweetened	53	75 ml	1 pint
Beetroot	30–40	120 gm	6 lb
Carrot	20	240 gm	4 lb
Parsnip	50	90 gm	3 lb
Potatoes	90	60 gm	
Glucose	318	10 gm	No
Honey	288	15 gm	more
Sucrose	394	10 gm	than will
Syrup	297	15 gm	give an
Treacle	257	15 gm	O.G. of 70
Bilberry	10 approx	Likely to be in	Up to 4 lb
Elder	10 approx	excess of 200 gm	Up to 4 lb

Artichoke

See Chapter 9; page 90.

Artichoke Wine

See Chapter 9; page 90.

Bilberry

A berry with the peculiar action of either causing or stopping diarrhoea! It is listed in some herbals as useful in diabetes, but there is no support for this in the pharmacopoeia.

Bilberry Wine

See Chapter 3; page 25.

Cabbage

This is said to lower the blood sugar. The juice of the white cabbage is listed in the pharmacopoeia as being effective in the treatment of stomach ulcers. There is no mention of any action against diabetes.

* Cabbage Wine

Ingredient	Quantity per gallon	Quantity per 5 litres
Cabbage	3½ lbs	1.75 kg
Dates	1 lb	500 gms
Orange	1	1
Lemon	1	1
Sugar	to SG 70	to SG 70
Yeast		
Vitamin B_1	6 mg	6 mg
Water	to volume	to volume

For the recommended additives, see Page 53.

Boil the cabbage with the stoned, chopped dates for ten minutes in 4 pints (2 litres) water with the lemon and orange (sliced). Strain and add the sugar. Allow to cool and add the nutrients and an active yeast starter. When fermentation dies down, make to volume, and ferment under air lock to dryness. Rack and mature in the usual way. Sweeten to taste as described in Chapter 5.

Carrot

A vegetable with a long list of herbal credits, from aiding many intestinal problems to ridding the body of excess fluid. It is claimed that carrots help reduce the blood sugar. However, there is no listing for them in the pharmacopoeia.

* Carrot Wine

Ingredient	Quantity per gallon	Quantity per 5 litres
Carrots	4 lbs	2 kg
White grape concentrate	$\frac{1}{2}$ pint	250 mls
Sugar	to SG 70	to SG 70
Yeast		
Vitamin B$_1$	6 mg	6 mg
Water	to volume	to volume

For the recommended additives, see Page 53.

Scrub the carrots, then peel and slice them. Boil in 4 pints (2 litres) water until they are soft. Strain the liquid over the sugar. When cool, add the grape concentrate, nutrients, and an active yeast starter. When fermentation dies down, make to volume, and ferment under air lock to dryness. Rack and mature in the usual way for at least one year. Sweeten to taste as described in Chapter 5.

Centaury

See Chapter 8; page 76.

Centaury Wine

See Chapter 8; page 77.

Coconut

Coconut appears in the pharmacopoeia as the base for various ointments and soaps. There is no mention of any diabetic action, although it is said by some herbals to lower the blood sugar.

★ Coconut Wine

Ingredient	Quantity per gallon	Quantity per 5 litres
Dessicated Coconut	1 lb	500 gms
Dates	1 lb	500 gms
Sugar	to SG 70	to SG 70
Yeast		
Vitamin B_1	6 mg	6 mg
Water	to volume	to volume

For the recommended additives, see Page 53.

Stone and chop the dates. Add them and the coconut to 4 pints (2 litres) of water and boil for fifteen minutes. Strain. Add the sugar and mix. When cool, add the nutrients and an active yeast starter. When fermentation dies down, make to volume, and ferment under air lock to dryness. Rack and mature in the usual way. Sweeten to taste as described in Chapter 5.

Dandelion

See Chapter 7; page 64.

Dandelion Wine

See Chapter 7; page 65.

Nettle

See Chapter 7; page 68.

Nettle Wine

See Chapter 7; page 68.

Spinach

While it is certain that this leaf contains significant amounts or iron, it is by no means safe to follow the claims that it is of value in diabetes. Possibly, the eating of a food low in carbohydrate plays a part in good diet, but more than that cannot be assumed.

✶   Spinach Wine

Ingredient	Quantity per gallon	Quantity per 5 litres
Spinach	3½ lbs	1.75 kg
Raisins	½ lb	250 gms
Sugar	to SG 70	to SG 70
Yeast		
Vitamin B$_1$	6 mg	6 mg
Water	to volume	to volume

For the recommended additives, see Page 53.

Wash and chop the raisins and spinach. Boil in 4 pints (2 litres) water for ten minutes. Strain the liquid over the sugar and mix. When cool, add the nutrients and an active yeast starter. When fermentation dies down, make to volume, and ferment under air lock to dryness. Rack and mature in the usual way. Sweeten to taste as described in Chapter 5.

14 Making a Sugar Free Beer

Although this chapter is aimed particularly at the diabetic brewer, the aims and solutions are essentially the same for the 'healthy' brewer. For the weight-conscious or merely careful drinker, all the points made, and recipes given later, are relevant and suitable to both.

There are now many commercially available beers for both diabetic and diet conscious drinker. They are all legally defined as *'Alcohol Free'* beers. In other words they all contain less than 2% of alcohol. For the diabetic drinker, the carbohydrate content is similarly low.

Despite this, beer drinking by diabetics remains a contentious subject. This is due to the greater quantity of calories and carbohydrate in beers which are not designated as *diabetic* by comparison with wines. (There are now available several 'alcohol free' wines as well as German wines specifically designated as diabetic.

In Table 15 there is a list of drinks and their portion size, calorific content, and the residual sugar per 100 ml.

The problem with making beers that are 'sugar-free' (and will suit the diabetic as well as ordinary drinker) is trying to eliminate the 'hidden calories' contained in the non-fermentable substances (such as dextrins), which are present in quantity in beers considered unfit for the diabetic. The beer we are trying to make must not contain excess alcohol while requiring body so that it is recognisable as a beer!

Dextrins contribute carbohydrate to a finished beer, and, like all carbohydrates, add to the calorific value. This does not matter in itself, since alcohol, residual sugar, and dextrins all contribute to the total calorific content. What we need to do is limit the overall content.

TABLE 15

Diabetic and other Beers

		Alcohol Content gm/ 100 ml	Residual Sugar gm/ 100 ml	Calories per 100 ml from		Total Calories per 100 ml	Calories per ½ pint
				Alcohol	Sugar		
Diabetic Beers	Henninger Diat Pils	4.77	0.7	33.39	2.63	36.02	106.92
	Marston's Low "C"	3.32	0.46	23.24	1.73	24.97	74.12
	Eldridge Konig Diabetic Lager	2.9	1.27	20.3	4.76	25.06	74.43
	Satzenbrau Diat Pils	4.9	0.75	34.3	2.81	37.1	113.6
	Holstein	4.48	0.7	31.36	2.63	33.99	107.92
	Whitbread	5.4	0.8	37.8	3	40.80	102
Beers	Brown Ale	2.24	2.95	15.68	11.06	26.74	79.52
	Bitter	3.07	2.25	21.49	8.44	29.93	88.04
	Mild Ale	2.6	1.61	18.2	6.04	24.24	71
	Pale Ale	3.34	1.99	23.38	7.46	30.84	90.88
	Stout	2.87	4.2	20.09	15.75	35.75	105.08
	Extra Stout	4.26	2.09	29.82	7.84	37.66	110.76
	Strong Ale	6.64	6.13	46.48	22.99	69.47	207.32
Cider	Cider, Dry	3.78	2.64	26.46	9.9	36.36	108.51
	Cider, Sweet	3.68	4.28	25.76	16.05	41.81	124.18
	Cider, Vintage	10.46	7.29	73.22	27.34	100.56	298.66

Carbohydrate in other forms is not so dangerous, provided the daily total is restricted.

The commercial diabetic beers are all based on worts which have little or no final carbohydrate. On the other hand, dextrins are important in the production of body in a beer, as well as aiding head retention.

Given that the wort must be limited in its original gravity, we find ourselves on the horns of a dilemma when we come to consider the alcohol content of a diabetic or healthy beer. In the ordinary course of events, the wort ferments out to its end point leaving a residuum of dextrins which, as we have seen, aid body and head retention in the finished beer. However, if we want a stronger beer,

147

we have to ensure a complete fermentation of dextrins to alcohol. This will result in a stronger beer with thin body.

As dextrins are only slowly fermentable, they are, if present, a source of what is, in effect, residual sugar. Thus, they will add to the carbohydrate content of a beer if it is drunk before the dextrins are fully converted.

When making grain beers it is most important to control the temperature and pH at which mashing is carried out, because the alpha and beta amylases which break down the malt to sugar and dextrins have different optima. By varying the conditions in the mash tun, it is possible to have a wort of differing composition according to preference, or in the case of the diabetic — necessity!

If the wort has an Original Gravity of 50 and mashing is carried out at a temperature of 145°F, (63°C), with a pH of 5, the resultant extract will have a fermentable composition of approximately 80% maltose and 20% dextrins. This, after fermentation, will give us a beer with about 4% alcohol with 3 gms per 100 mls residual sugar (16.5 gms per pint). This works out that the beer has about 210 calories per pint (200 calories per 500 mls), made up of 150 calories from the alcohol and 60 from the dextrins.

If all the starch in the grain was converted to maltose, the final beer would have a composition of 6% alcohol with no dextrins, and have the same calorific content. However, although conforming to the diabetic rules of carbohydrate restriction, the beer will, as we have seen, be thin with poor head retention.

When making a 'sugar free' beer for the diabetic or health conscious, the danger is that one can easily forget the calories and carbohydrate by the dextrins. Thus, the figures worked out for the beer will give only 80% of the true calorific and 20% of the correct carbohydrate content.

In order to avoid falling into this trap, calculate the calorific value of the beer from the gravity. This figure is obtained by taking the SG of the wort. From the gravity tables work out the sugar content in grams per 250 mls. This figure, multiplied by 7 gives the approximate calorific content of the beer per pint. While this is an over estimation, it is better, and safer from the diatetic point of view, to over rather than under estimate the figure.

Above all else, do not aim for great strength in your beers. Make weaker beers and concentrate on flavour. Do not add any sugar (such as priming sugar) beyond that obtained from mashing or malt extract.

148

For a beer to have good body it needs to contain dextrins, and, a palatable beer requires at least *some* alcohol in it!

To achieve a happy medium between flat, thin, tasteless drinks, and a good beer, it is important to try to arrive at a compromise in recipe formulation between the high carbohydrate commercials and the thin 'diabetic' beers with 'no' carbohydrate. The first, and most important, point to make about commercial diabetic beers is that they are all much stronger than their 'normal' counterparts. If one takes an average alcohol content by weight, one gets an average content of 4.3 gms per 100 mls for all the diabetic beers listed in Table 147.

This compares with an average for all commercial beers, including 'strong ales' of 3.57 gms per 100 mls. Remove the strong ales and stout from the calculation, and a figure of 3.06 gms% alcohol is obtained.

This last figure compares well with the suggested limit of 3% alcohol for our 'diabetic' and healthy beers as being a suitable figure at which to aim.

So, do not be misled by any advertising campaign which suggests that commercial diabetic beers are entirely safe to drink. Or that one can drink and drive with them.

The most noticeable comment heard from beer drinkers who try diabetic beers is that there 'is nothing to them'. However, despite the lack of body and taste, after four or five halves, they frequently find themselves on the floor! This is followed the next morning by an appalling hang-over! This is easily explained by the lack of body, and, to my palate, lack of taste. This means that, without exercising great care, the diabetic is easily led into consuming excessive quantities.

It is interesting to note that only a few of the commercially available diabetic beers contain warnings on the label that they are not suitable for the over-weight or those on a diet. To my mind, this statement should apply automatically to a diabetic; for, although he is not necessarily on a strict calorie-controlled diet, he should nevertheless be extremely aware and conscious of his total intake. It is not, or rather should not, be simply carbohydrate that is being monitored.

To my mind, those diabetics who want to drink outside their own homes could well choose to drink smaller quantities of alcohol — both in terms of calorie, as well as alcohol content — whilst enjoying the better taste of 'ordinary' beer. In order to do this, simply adjust the carbohydrate intake to allow for the content in ordinary beer.

From Tables 10 and 15, it is obvious that beer comes far worse than wines when considered in normal drinking quantities. Wine contains about 70 calories per portion, while beer contains between 150-200 per pint. In order to correct this imbalance, it is necessary to lower the alcohol content of diabetic and healthy beers by a proportionally greater amount than similar wines. On the whole, it is probably best, in the interest of diabetic dietary control, to place a limit of 3% (115 calories per pint), on any diabetic beer. This means that many of the usual beers can be emulated with some degree of success.

In the interest of flavour, it is best to stick to mild and bitter beers, together with lagers. Stouts, on the whole, benefit from greater strength.

To make a malt extract beer, it is simple to prepare a wort according to the simple recipes and follow the steps listed. Making grain beers involves mashing, the process whereby the crushed grain is mixed with water at a carefully controlled temperature, in order to extract the starch and convert it into a fermentable form. By varying the mashing temperature, the proportion of dextrins and nitrogenous materials extracted will vary. The precise temperature is not as critical as was thought formerly, but, a reasonable degree of control is needed.

When making normal grain beers, mashing is carried out at a temperature of betweeen 145-150°F, (62-65°C). This, as we have seen, results in a wort with a composition of about 80% maltose and 20% dextrins. However, we wish to reduce the dextrins in order to reduce the carbohydrate content. To do this, we need to have as much activity as possible from the alpha amylase group of enzymes responsible for the breakdown of starch to dextrins. Beta amylase, on the other hand, breaks down starch to maltose — as well as dextrins to maltose. This enzyme has an optimum temperature of 130°F, (54°C), at which it works with the greatest efficiency. The pH should be 4.7. (This contrasts with the optima for alpha amylase of 150°F, (65°C) at a pH of 5.7.

In order to achieve our aim of making a beer without dextrins, we, therefore, need to ensure the conversion of as much of the dextrins as possible. This may be done by mashing at a temperature of 130-135°F (54-57°C), in a pH which is on the acid side of neutral. The resultant wort should have a good extract with little in the way of non-fermentable carbohydrate in it.

Another advantage of the low mashing temperature is that the barley can have a comparatively high nitrogen content, but, since the enzymes present at that temperature break down protein, the finished beer should not have a protein haze. The proteins that remain are helpful in head formation — thus helping to overcome the disadvantage of a low dextrin beer. However, to make a true British Bitter, one has the problem that the beer requires to have more body than the continental type lagers. Because bitters need time to mature, they require a modicum of sugar to ensure condition as well as helping to counteract the bitterness of the hops. This now means that a bitter has to contain extra carbohydrate which should, from the diabetic viewpoint, be anathema. But provided the original gravity is kept below 30, I see no reason why the moderate consumption of a bitter should not be permissable to a diabetic — provided the carbohydrate contained therein is allowed for in the daily dietary calculations.

Basically, therefore, when making a diabetic beer, any beer recipe can be used. But, it must be adjusted to give an Original Gravity of 30 (SG 1030).

Do not add any priming sugar after fermentation beyond the amount specified in the recipe.

Any unfermented dextrins present in a bitter will, during maturation, be gradually partly converted into fermentable maltose which will prove a sufficient source of priming sugar. Do not forget that this stage will take a lot longer than if using priming sugar. So, to allow for this, always mature diabetic beers as though they were lagers. It is also useful to use heading liquids to aid head retentions, in case dextrins and protein are lacking. A situation which would result in a beer lacking in condition.

If the beer is made from a low dextrin malt, it may need sweetening. Again, if dextrins are present, and not broken down, they will confer some sweetness to the beer. If, however, the beer is not sweet enough, do not add extra sugar. Instead, sweeten it as described in Chapter 5.

Beers such as those described in this Chapter may seem apallingly non-alcoholic. They are no more so than many accepted commercial brews.

If malt alone is used to make the beer, avoiding 'sugar' such as household, the beer will have a far better flavour and body. This will make up for many of the shortcomings due to the lack of alcohol.

To repeat what I said at the beginning of the chapter — do not aim to make anaesthetics. Aim for weaker, but more flavoursome beers.

TABLE 16

Equivalent Sugar Extracted from Brewing Ingredients

Cane Sugar	100%
The darker sugars are 2 or 3% less but this is not material	
Invert Sugar	80% (water of crystallisation)
Malt Extract	80%
Pale Malt	70%
Crystal Malt	70%
Flaked Barley	70%
Flaked Maize and Rice	80%
Brewing Flour	85%
Wheat Malt	75% (huskless)

15 Sugar Free Beer Recipes

Although most commercial beers have original gravities of around 30, there are very few recipes for homemade beers with O.G.s below 35. This is, as we have already seen, too high for either diabetic or 'healthy beers'; our O.G. has to be about 30.

It is, in fact, extremely easy to adjust any recipe that catches your fancy to bring the original gravity down to the required limit. When doing this, it is best to reduce the sugar content appropriately by adjusting the starting gravity to 29. This leaves 'space' for priming sugar to ensure condition in the finished beer.

Although brewing grain beers is becoming increasingly popular, using malt extract as a base ingredient simplifies the art of brewing. The first figure needed is the amount of fermentable extract a unit weight of each ingredient will add to a wort. Table 17 shows the approximate yields.

From the table, you can see that malt extract will give an expected yield of 80% compared to sucrose. Since 1 lb of sugar dissolved in 1 gallon of water has an S.G. of 39, it follows that 1 lb of malt extract will have an S.G. of 31.2 in the same volume.

When formulating a recipe, add up the specific gravities that each ingredient will contribute to the wort. This figure is then divided by the intended volume to give the S.G. per gallon.

To give an example: Let us make 4 gallons of bitter with an O.G. of 30, using malt extract. If we use 3 lbs of malt extract, this will yield 0.8 × 3, or 2.4 units of gravity. If we divide by the number of gallons being made, and then multiply by 39 (the gravity of 1 lb of sugar), we get an O.G. of 23 — which is too low.

Therefore, to try the same calculation with 4 lbs of extract which gives 3.2 units of gravity. Again, dividing by the intended volume, and multiplying by the S.G. of sugar, we get 31.2 for the original gravity.

TABLE 17

Maximum Quantities of Brewing Ingredients used alone — Amount per Gallon or 5 Litres.

Ingredient	Quantity	Equivalent to sugar	OG
Malt Extract Flaked Maize Rice	15 oz (500 gms)	80%	30
Pale Malt Crystal Malt Flaked Barley	17 oz (510 gms)	70%	30
Brewing Flour	14 oz (420 gms)	85%	30
Wheat Malt	16 oz (480 gms)	75%	30

In fact, 3 lbs 12 oz will give a gravity of 29.25, which is accurate enough for our purposes. Particularly if using the same calculation on a grain beer, since the extract is rarely 100 per cent. In practice, of course, one rarely uses only one ingredient. The principle of the calculation remains the same.

When making an extract beer, all that is required is to place the ingredients in a boiler and boil for 45 minutes. Strain the wort and allow to cool before adding an active yeast starter.

The simplest formulation for an extract beer working within the limits imposed is as follows for 5 gallons (or 25 litres).

Simple Malt Extract Bitter

Malt Extract	2 lbs
Sugar	3 lbs
or	
Malt Extract	1 lbs
Sugar	1½ lbs
Hops	1-2 oz depending on personal taste. Probably best to use are *Goldings*.

However, a beer like this will tend to be thin bodied and have poor retention and condition. In order to improve these, grain of some sort is advisable.

∗ Light Ale – O.G. 30

Ingredient	Quantity per 5 gallons	Quantity per 25 litres
Malt extract	4 lbs	1750 gms
White priming sugar	1 oz	30 gms
Golding hops	1.5-2 oz	45–60 gms
Beer Yeast		
Water Treatment	as needed	as needed
Water	to volume	to volume

Add the extract and sugar to 2 gallons (10 litres) of boiling water. Bring to the boil, add the hops and boil for 30 minutes. Place in a plastic bucket and make up to final volume.

Check the pH with pH papers and adjust with water treatment if required to make the pH as near 4.8 as possible.

Allow to cool before pitching an active yeast starter. Skim off the first head that forms and then allow to ferment to a gravity of 7. (S.G. 1.007).

Rack and bottle using the permitted amount of sugar to prime the bottles.

Alow to mature for at least four or five days.

✳ **Mild – O.G. 30**

Ingredient	Quantity per 5 gallons	Quantity per 25 litres
Diastatic malt extract	3 lbs	1350 gms
Crystal malt	8 oz	250 gms
Black malt	4 oz	125 gms
Soft brown sugar	12 oz	375 gms
Fuggles hops	2 oz	60 gms
Salt	$\frac{1}{6}$ oz	5 gms
Irish moss	$\frac{1}{30}$ oz	1 gm
Beer Yeast		
Water treatment	as needed	as needed
Water	to volume	to volume

Boil all ingredients except the sugar for half an hour in $1\frac{1}{2}$ gallons of water. Then strain the wort onto the sugar. Make up to volume. Allow to cool to 70°F (21°C) before pitching an active yeast starter.

Ferment to 1009 and rack to a bulk container to mature for at least one week before priming and bottling.

✳ **Light Bitter – O.G. 30**

Ingredient	Quantity per 5 gallons	Quantity per 25 litres
Diastatic malt extract	3 lbs	1350 gms
Cracked crystal malt	4 oz	125 gms
Glucose chips	1lb 8 oz	650 gms
Goldings hops	3 oz	90 gms
Beer yeast		
Water treatment	as needed	as needed
Water	to volume	to volume

Boil all the ingredients for one hour. Make up to final volume and allow to cool before pitching an active yeast starter.

Allow to ferment to a gravity of 7. Then continue as outlined in the previous recipe for maturing and bottling.

* ## Light Lager – O.G. 30

Ingredient	Quantity per 5 gallons	Quantity per 25 litres
Malt extract	4 lbs 6 oz	2 kilos
Hallertau hops	2 oz	60 gms
Citric acid	$\frac{1}{2}$ teaspoon	2.5 gms
Lager yeast		
Water treatment	as needed	as needed
Water	to volume	to volume

First ensure that your water is soft. If not treat it to soften it before boiling the extract and hops in 2 gallons of water for half an hour. Make up to volume and allow to cool before pitching an active yeast starter.

Allow to ferment until the S.G. is 1010. At this point, rack the beer into a bulk container with air lock. After one week, rack, prime and bottle in the usual manner.

* ## Bitter – O.G. 30

Ingredient	Quantity per 5 gallons	Quantity per 25 litres
Crushed pale malt	4 lbs	2 kilos
Flaked maize	8 oz	250 gms
Torrified barley	4 oz	125 gms
Glucose chips	1 lb	500 gms
White sugar	2 oz	60 gms
Fuggles hops	1 oz	30 gms
Hop extract	1 oz	30 gms
Irish moss	1 teaspoon	5 gms
Gelatine	$\frac{1}{2}$ oz	15 gms
Beer yeast		
Water treatment	as needed	as needed
Water	to volume	to volume

After treating the water to harden it so that it is suitable for bitter brewing, raise the temperature to 140°F (60°C). Stir in the crushed malt, flakes and grain. Stirring continuously, slowly raise the temperature to 150°F (66°C). Allow the mash to rest for two hours, heating the mixture slightly if the temperature falls. Then sparge the mash. To do this, place the mixture in a large grain bag. Then slowly run treated water through at a temperature of about 160°F (70°C). Continue the process until you have collected approximately 4 gallons (20 litres) of sweet wort.

Now, add the hops and glucose chips and boil the wort for one and a half hours. Using Irish moss during the last 30 minutes of the boil will aid clarity.

Strain the wort off the hops into a fermenting vat and make up to volume with cold (but treated) water. When cool, add an active yeast starter and the hop extract.

Ferment for 4-5 days, until the S.G. has fallen to 1010, and rack into either one or two gallon (5 or 10 litre) demijohns. Add the gelatine to aid fining. Allow to mature for one week before racking into a pressure barrel together with the priming sugar. Allow to condition for three or four days before sampling.

✱ Pale Ale – O.G. 30

Ingredient	Quantity per 5 gallons	Quantity per 25 litres
Crushed pale malt	4 lb 8 oz	2250 gms
Flaked maize	14 oz	450 gms
Invert sugar	12 oz	400 gms
Fuggles hops	3 oz	100 gms
Irish moss	1 teaspoon	5 gms
Gelatine	$\frac{1}{2}$ oz	15 gms
Brown Sugar	2 oz	60 gms
Beer yeast		
Water treatment	as needed	as needed
Water	to volume	to volume

Treat the water to make it suitable for pale ale. Then raise the temperature to 140°F (60°C). Stir in the crushed malt and flakes. Stirring continuously, raise the temperature to 150°F (66°C).

Leave for one and a half hours, bringing the temperature up to 160°F occasionally.

Sparge the grist by placing the mash in a grain bag and washing it with water (again treated if necessary), at a temperature of 158°F (70°C). Collect a total of 4 gallons (20 litres) of wort.

Add the hops and boil for one and a half hours. Dissolve the majority of the sugar, and add it during the boil. Also, add the Irish moss towards the end of the boiling period.

Strain the wort off the hops, make to volume with cold treated water, and when cool, pitch an active yeast starter.

From here, the method is the same as for the previous bitter recipe. (Page 157).

✳ Special Mild – O.G. 31

Ingredient	Quantity per 5 gallons	Quantity per 25 litres
Crushed pale malt	4 lbs 8 oz	2200 gms
Crushed black malt	6 oz	200 gms
Soft brown sugar	1 lb 2 oz	560 gms
Black treacle	2 oz	60 gms
Fuggles hops	1 oz	30 gms
Hop extract	1½ oz	50 gms
Gelatine	½ oz	15 gms
Saccharine tablets	5	5
Beer yeast		
Water treatment	as needed	as needed
Water	to volume	to volume

Heat 2½ gallons (12.5 litres) of correctly treated water 140°F (60°C). Stir in the crushed grains. Raise the temperature to 150°F (66°C), stirring all the time. Keep it at this level for one and a half hours. Then sparge the mash – as described in previous recipes – to collect 4 gallons (20 litres) of wort. Boil the wort with the hops for one hour before adding the treacle and all the sugar except for two ounces, (60 gms), which must be kept for priming, and the Irish Moss. Continue the boiling for a further thirty minutes before straining into a fermentation container.

Make up to volume with cold treated water; add an active yeast starter when the wort is at the correct temperature (about 70°F [21°C]). Ferment until the gravity has fallen to 1010. Rack into bulk containers with the gelatine finings. Fit air locks and allow to continue fermentation for another seven days before racking into primed bottles or pressure barrel (the better for this recipe) using the sugar kept back from the recipe.

Allow to condition for five days before sampling.

∗ Sweet Stout – O.G. 30

Ingredient	Quantity per 3 gallons	Quantity per 15 litres
S.F.X. malt extract	2 lbs	1200 gms
Crushed chocolate malt	4 oz	125 gms
Brewer's caramel	4 teaspoons	20 mls
Soft brown sugar	1 lb	500 gms
Fuggles hops	1 oz	30 gms
Northern brewer hops	1 oz	30 gms
Saccharin tablets	5	5
White sugar	2 oz	60 gms
Beer yeast		
Water treatment	as needed	as needed
Water	to volume	to volume

Add the malt extract, grains and hops to 2 gallons (10 litres) of treated water. Boil for 45 minutes. Then, carefully strain the wort off the hops and spent grains into a fermentation vat. Rinse the grain and hops with two kettles of hot water to extract the last of the sugar. Dissolve the caramel and brown sugar in hot water (again, ensure that it has been treated if necessary), and add to the fermentation vat.

Make to volume and allow to cool to 70°F (21°C), before pitching an active yeast starter. Add the saccharin tablets (or 5 drops of liquid if you prefer). Ferment for four to five days and rack to bulk containers under air lock for a further seven days.

Rack the beer into primed bottles using the white sugar at a rate of ½ a teaspoon per pint (½ litre) bottle. Allow at least ten days maturation before drinking.

✳ Lager – O.G. 30

Ingredient	Quantity per 5 gallons	Quantity per 25 litres
Crushed lager malt	4½ lbs	2125 gms
Flaked maize	14 oz	400 gms
Crushed wheat malt	9 oz	250 gms
Hallertau hops	2 oz	60 gms
Irish moss	1 teaspoon	5 gms
Gelatine finings	½ oz	15 gms
Beer yeast		
Water treatment	as needed	as needed
Water	to volume	to volume

After treating the water, if necessary, heat 2½ gallons (12.5 litres) to 113°F (45°C). Stir in the crushed malts and flakes, and continue to stir while raising the temperature to 131°F (55°C). Keep the temperature at this level for half an hour and then raise the temperature to 150°F (66°C). Maintain this temperature for one hour before sparging as described in previous recipes. Collect a total of 4 gallons (20 litres) of wort.

Add the hops and boil the wort for one hour. Next add the Irish moss and continue the boil for a further thirty minutes.

Strain the wort into the fermentation vat; make to volume with cold treated water. When the wort temperature has fallen to about 70°F (21°C), add an active yeast starter.

Ferment until the gravity has fallen to 1010. Then rack into gallon jars with the gelatine finings, and allow to continue like this for three weeks.

Rack the beer into bottles, using the white sugar as priming. The beer will need at least three weeks in bottle before it has enough condition to drink.

16 Your Very Good Health

If, after all this, it is still allowed to enjoy a drink, how much can one drink, and of what? Let us start by emphasising those who *should not* take alcohol.

Anyone taking tranquilisers must not drink. Many other medicines, also, mean that alcohol must be avoided while taking them. If in doubt, ask your doctor or pharmacist for advice.

During pregnancy, it is safest not to drink.

The diabetic whose condition is controlled by tablets must be extra cautious about alcohol. Some of the pills can, if alcohol is taken, actually cause a rise in the blood sugar. These pills include *Chlorpromazine, Tolazamide, Tolbutamide, Phenformin,* and *Metformin.* If your diabetes goes awry after even one drink, it is worth checking that it is not the pills making the problem worse.

Medical conditions in which alcohol are taboo include liver disease because alcohol causes liver damage. The alcoholic must never drink; not only is his or her liver in danger, but other organs like the brain can also be irreversibly damaged.

If during the course of an illness your doctor forbids alcohol, heed his instructions. There will be good reason behind the 'orders'.

As we discussed earlier, the maximum recommended weekly intake should not exceed fourteen drinks. And the daily limit is three. In the chapter on *gout,* we saw how the uric acid level is raised if two drinks are taken every day. Hence, the modern notion that, not only should there be a daily and weekly limit, but also, you should have at least two days per week without alcohol. This is, literally, to allow the liver to recover itself. Another thing to avoid is a 'binge'. Apart from the unpleasantness of a hangover, they, too, can cause gout.

When making your own wines, make sure that you only use safe species. Any plant that is in any way dubious must not be used. Many plants used in herbal treatments are, in fact poisonous. Using them correctly is an art that takes many years to learn. Do not try to make wines from any such plants. Most chapters have a list of *some* of the poisonous plants to be found in herbals. These lists are by no means exhaustive. If in doubt about the safety of a plant **do not use it.**

With all this in mind, enjoy a 'sugar-free' beer or wine. The reduced alcohol levels which have been advocated will reduce calorific content; as will sweetening with artificial sweeteners.

All this should mean that the enjoyment of a drink will do no harm. Hopefully, the herbal bases for the wines will even enhance good health.

However, to repeat another warning. Do not think that twice the dose of any medicine will do twice as much good. Frequently, this will do actual harm.

Without repeating the entire book, the maxim has to be — *moderation in all things, especially moderation.*

SELECT BIBLIOGRAPHY

Among the books used as references, the following is a selection of those that may prove of most interest.

Alcoholic, The, and the Help he needs Max Glatt.
Arthritis & Folk Medicine D. C. Jarvis.
Biological Principles of Fermentation J. G. Carr.
Brewer's Dictionary Peter McCall (Argus Books).
British Pharmacopoeia 1890.
British Pharmacopoeia 25th Edition.
Culpeper's Complete Herbal reprinted by Foulsham.
Diabetic Beer & Winemaking Peter McCall (Argus Books).
Recipes for Diabetics Billie Little.
Dictionary of Modern Herbalism, The Simon Y. Mills.
Good Food, Gluten Free Hilda Cherry Hills.
Herb Book, The Peter Lust.
How to Wine Your Way to Good Health Herbert M. Baus.
Modern Herbal, A Mrs. M. Grieve.
Plants Unsafe for Winemaking Edwin Belt.
Poisonous Plants and Fungi Pamela North.
Preserving Winemaking Ingredients Edwin Belt.
Progressive Winemaking B. Acton and P. Duncan.
Recipes for Prizewinning Wines B. Acton.
Roots of Health Leon Petulengro.
Sugar & Health World Sugar Research.
Sugar is GOOD for you Sugar Research Council.
Theriac & Mithradatum Gilbert Watson.
Vegetable, Herb & Cereal Wines T. E. Belt (Foremost).
Wild Plants for Winemaking Edwin Belt.
Wine is the Best Medicine E. A. Maury.
Wine & Your Well Being Salvatore Lucia.
Winemaker's Dictionary Peter McCall (Argus Books).
Winemaking the Natural Way Ian Ball.
What's Your Poison Paul Gwinner & Marcus Grant.
Wine Diet Cookbook Salvatore Lucia and Emily Chase.

Index

166

Eat Drink and be Healthy

SAVE £5

Take out a year's subscription to Here's Health, Britain's best selling health magazine and you will save £5 on the normal price. All you have to do is to complete the coupon below and send your remittance for £13.50 and you will receive every month for the next year a copy of Here's Health sent direct to your home. Send the completed coupon to Here's Health Subscriptions, Infonet, 5 River Park Industrial Estate, Berkhamsted, Herts. HP4 1HL

Please send me the next 12 issues of Here's Health every month to the address below

NAME ....

ADDRESS ....

....

....POSTCODE ....

SIGNATURE ....

DATE ....

☐   I enclose my cheque/postal order payable to Here's Health for £13.50

☐   Please charge my Access/Barclay card account

No. ☐☐☐☐☐☐☐☐☐☐☐☐☐☐☐☐☐☐

the sum of £13.50

Ref. Healthy Wine & Beer Making

Here's Health